Macramé

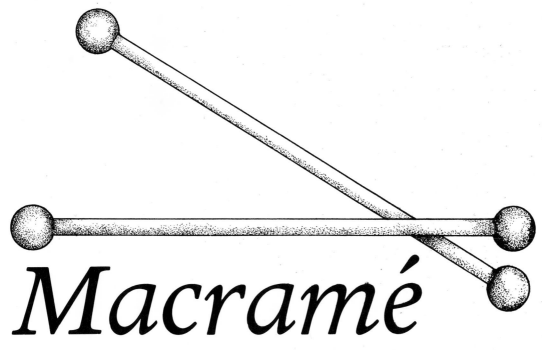

Macramé

A Comprehensive Guide

Heidy Willsmore

with drawings by Peggy Tasker
and photographs by Andrew de Lory

FABER & FABER   LONDON & BOSTON

First published in 1979
by Faber and Faber Ltd
3 Queen Square London WC1
Filmset and printed in Great Britain by
BAS Printers Limited, Over Wallop, Hampshire
All rights reserved.

British Library Cataloguing in Publication Data

Willsmore, Heidy
  Macramé.
  1. Macramé
  I. Title
  746.4   TT840

ISBN 0-571-11310-9

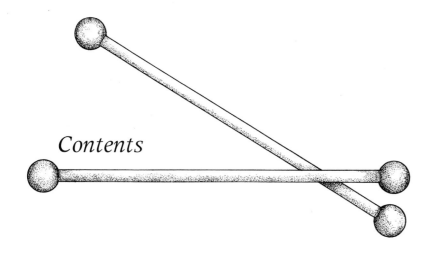

Contents

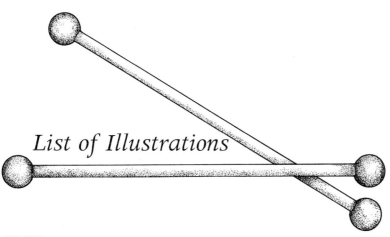

List of Illustrations

COLOUR

A Chinese-type lantern in fine cotton twine and wrought-iron flower trough covered with a pattern in two colours

B Tiffany lampshade with matching jar covered in turquoise dish-cloth cotton. Three examples of Cavandoli work

C Wall hangings in jute with curved lines based on the Art Nouveau style, and with fish design inspired by a painting of Paul Klee's

D Oval design with beads and Macramé-edged mirror. Handbag with matching belt in cotton twine

E Wrought-iron firescreen covered in a three-colour pattern. Sculptured head in natural cotton twine

F A selection of knotted belts

G Abstract hanging in three colours worked in jute and natural materials. Large plant pot hanger in thick jute

H Wall hanging in bleached and brown jute and matching lampshade in brown, beige and white wool

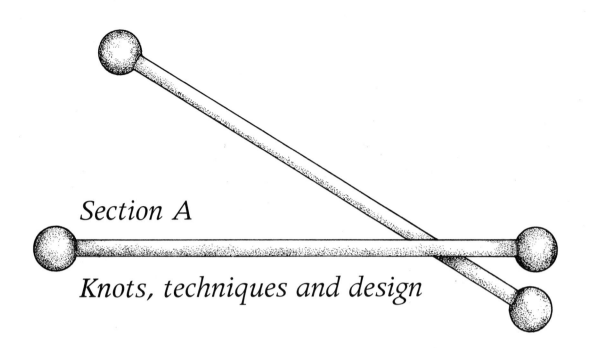

Section A

Knots, techniques and design

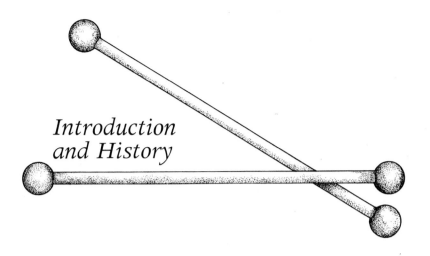

Introduction
and History

Few crafts can claim to be as fascinating, absorbing and versatile as Macramé, and yet it is not practised as widely as some. The reason why this ancient form of knotting is still unknown to many lies in the fact that it has a habit of going in and out of fashion. The unusual name which is said to be derived from the Arabic word 'Migramah', meaning fringes, gives no indication as to the actual nature of the work and until one becomes enlightened on the subject could well be regarded as a French dish or the name of a mystical figure.

The knot itself is, of course, prehistoric and was initially used for functional purposes only. Some of the earliest evidence of decorative knotting dates back to Assyrian times and finds in tombs have revealed that similar knots to those used in Macramé today were known to the Egyptians. Certain forms of knotting, like heavy fringes, are said to have been worked in Arabia since the thirteenth century. Knotted lace was made in France during the fourteenth century and similarly by the Italians in the Renaissance period. The popularity of this kind of lace spread rapidly through Europe. It is believed that Macramé was introduced to England by Queen Mary, wife of William of Orange, in the seventeenth century, having learned it in Holland. During the late Georgian era Queen Charlotte, wife of King George III, is known to have made knotted fringes at court. The art of Macramé enjoyed particular popularity in late Victorian times when elaborate trimmings for fireplaces, four-poster beds and shelves were made.

Sailors have contributed enormously to spreading the art of knotting all over the world. The ropes and decorative articles worked during their long voyages were often used for barter at the various ports. Examples of sailors' work can be seen at maritime museums. Today's revival of Macramé is largely due to fashion and differs from earlier forms inasmuch as many decorative pieces are worked in much coarser yarns to suit present-day trends and taste. A large variety of natural and synthetic materials in many thicknesses are available now, enabling us to produce all kinds of interesting textures.

A representative collection of work, ranging from lace-like to coarse fabrics, is shown in this book which I have tried to write bearing in mind the particular needs and problems students have in class. It contains not only a comprehensive course in Macramé, both elementary and more advanced, but also useful hints and working techniques. Furthermore, you will find guidance on design, where to look for it and how to go about it, with illustrations to substantiate the various facts given. The book also provides a section on items to make, both practical and decorative, with full working instructions. There is, however, no reason why readers should not, in time, design their own pieces of work once acquainted with this most fascinating and rewarding pastime.

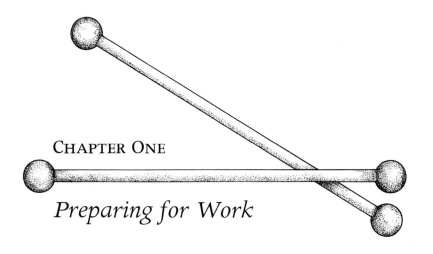

CHAPTER ONE

Preparing for Work

The basic requirements for Macramé work

The tools necessary for Macramé work are very few. The knotting is done simply by using your fingers and no needles or other instruments are needed. However, in order to achieve a high standard of work it is essential to have a good-sized, solid base to work on. For this purpose a piece of insulation board 20 × 16 in (50 × 50 cm) is recommended, soft enough to take pins. These can be obtained from most wood yards. Subdivide the board into 1-in (2½-cm) squares using a thick felt pen. Mark the squares along the longer top edge from 1 to 20 and the shorter side edge from 1 to 16 (or both edges from 1 to 20 when working in metres). The lines will help you to knot accurately and the numbered sides may serve as a measure, the 20 and 16 in (50 and 50 cm) together making up one yard (one metre). The metric board is slightly larger. Smaller boards tend to lift off and move about the working surface when knotting.

In addition, you will need pins to hold your work in place. Ordinary dressmaking pins with large glass heads are ideal for this and less likely to hurt your fingers than pins with steel heads. There are special T-shaped pins for Macramé work on the market which are very strong and may be useful for securing big or heavy pieces to the board. In the ordinary way, however, the cords seem to catch rather easily on their fairly large heads. The more frequently you pin your knotting the more accurate it will become.

Yarn, scissors and possibly a tape measure are all that is required now before work may begin. The basic list of tools, therefore, looks as follows:
Knotting board 20 × 16 in (50 × 50 cm), Pins with large glass heads, Scissors, Yarn, Tape Measure (unless board is used). According to the project in hand you may find a need for a number of additional items such as fabric glue for concealing string ends at the back of work. Needles with eyes of varying sizes can be useful for sewing in ends or putting cords through confined spaces. Other aids and helpful items are mentioned under 'Accessories' (see page 87).

Yarns

Naturally, you will choose yarns suitable for the articles which you plan to make. Anything from the very finest crochet cotton (giving a lace-like effect) to the roughest jute or sisal (producing a coarse, rustic look) can be used. Some materials lend themselves better for certain purposes than others. One of the most fascinating aspects of Macramé is to experiment with various yarns, thereby producing many different effects. You will enjoy the thicker cords for quickness, the thin yarns for intricacy, wool perhaps for its softness and kind touch to your fingers. Each material has its own special merit.

WHERE TO LOOK FOR YOUR YARNS

A list of suppliers is mentioned in the back of this book but parcel string may be obtained from stationers and ironmongers, jute from gardening shops, wools, rug wool, cottons and dish-cloth cotton as well as gold and silver novelty yarns from woolshops and department stores. Specialist craft shops and sometimes ship's chandlers have interesting yarns and cords to offer. Some of the materials specially produced for Macramé work are very highly priced and it is well worth looking for bargains wherever you happen to be. Sales are a good time for wools, etc. Plastic-covered or plastic-type yarns are difficult to work with unless they are kept in a very warm place which makes them more pliable.

WHERE TO KNOT

The ideal working place is not always what we have available in our homes. Some materials shed a certain amount of fluff and small bits, particularly jute and sisal. I would, therefore, not advise knotting to take place in the kitchen unless you can have a thorough clean-up

18

between knotting and preparing your meals. Having a work room, thereby keeping the rest of your home respectable, would be an advantage. If you do not have this facility it may help to spread an old sheet over the floor where you are sitting. This should catch most of the bits and can be shaken out from time to time. Work at a table, if possible, and protect it with a table cloth or similar. Pins have a habit of finding their way between your table and the knotting board which can cause rather bad damage. You should sit straight in front of your work in good light. Knotting in an uncomfortable position may result in backache.

Should you eventually take on bigger projects it would be desirable to have a large sheet of insulation board which can be stood up against a wall. You then place yourself in front of it, knotting at a convenient level and the piece of work can be moved up at intervals to a comfortable working height. This also has the advantage that the entire worked area as an overall picture is in front of you, making it easier to decide on patterns and proportions as the project progresses.

Length of cords

Anyone writing a book on Macramé would prefer to ignore this subject, I am sure. Assessing the required lengths of cords is, without a doubt, the most difficult aspect of the craft. A rough guideline is

8 times the length of the finished article if the pattern is to be kept simple and all cords do a similar amount of work,
9–10 times the length of the finished article if the pattern is to be a more closely knotted one with a fair amount of Cording,
For a very dense pattern still more yarn may be necessary.

With some exceptions, strands are normally folded in half before mounting, as explained under 'Setting on cords' on page 20. The measurements above are for cords which will be mounted in this way.

For long Sinnets (see page 32) i.e. dog leads, covering light flexes or coat hangers, etc. with yarn, the Working Cords (each single cord-end) must be about $6\frac{1}{2}$ to 7 times the length of the Filler Cords or flex, etc. or longer still if the item to be covered is very thick.

Many factors affect the correct assessment of lengths of yarns and experience will show that according to the pattern some strands will do far more work than others. Thicker yarns are used up more quickly than thinner ones. When following set working instructions this will obviously be allowed for. Even the most experienced knotter will have to join in new lengths of cord at certain stages.

KEEP A RECORD

It is most helpful to keep a record of the requirements used for any particular piece of work. Once the quantities for a certain item are known, calculations for pieces to be made up in the same or similar material should be much easier. The yarn lengths could, for instance, be doubled if your work is to be twice as long. I myself do not simply keep a record of the quantities of yarn cut; a typical entry in my notebook might read:

BAG IN NATURAL COTTON TWINE (WORKED IN THREE PANELS)

Back and front alike:
    38 cords, each 90 in (2.20 m) long,
    2 side cords, each 110 in (2.80 m) long.
    (cords on centre panel ran short—add an extra 10 in (25 cm) next time)

This allows for the adjustment of measurements in the future and gives a fairly reliable guideline for any of my students who wish to make a similar item. The working tension varies from person to person and this can affect the lengths of cords quite considerably. If it is obvious in advance that certain strands will do more work than others, extra yarn may be allowed to counteract this. It is sometimes possible to set on cords unevenly, as is shown under 'Making a Sampler' (see page 124). A notebook and pencil are invaluable for this reason.

Setting on cords (Fig. 1)
When a piece of work is started, cords have to be set onto what is known as a 'Knot Bearer'. This can be a wooden stick, bamboo cane, metal rod or a piece of cord, etc. In the latter instance we also refer to the 'Holding Cord'. The knot bearer must, of course, be long enough to take the required number of strands comfortably. In the case of wooden or other rigid knot bearers pin these in position on your board either with pins above and below the rod or with U-pins making sure that the cords, once set on, do not slide off the ends. When setting strands onto a piece of cord, as one would do for bags (unless handles of another material, such as wood, are used), table mats, cushions, etc., pin this in place as shown below, using an Overhand Knot at either end (see Fig. 1) to secure firmly. In either case make sure that the knot bearer or holding cord is pinned to the board at a convenient working level and preferably along one of the marked lines for accuracy. The work can be moved up as it progresses.

Lark's Head Knot (Figs. 2–5)
This knot is most commonly used for setting on cords.

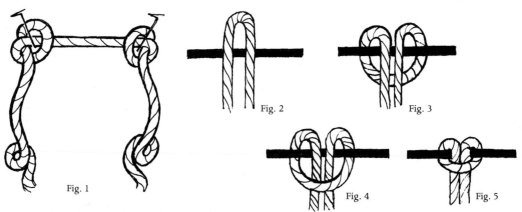

Fig. 1

Fig. 2

Fig. 3

Fig. 4

Fig. 5

Inverted Lark's Head Knot (Figs. 6–9)
The inverted Lark's Head Knot is an ordinary Lark's Head Knot worked back to front and is sometimes preferable when no loops are meant to be seen.

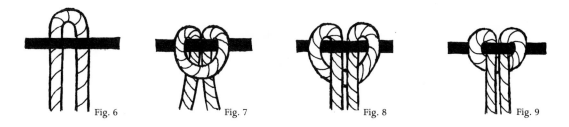

Fig. 6   Fig. 7   Fig. 8   Fig. 9

Provided your knot bearer is open ended a quick way of setting on cords when working with long strands is to form a Lark's Head Knot with your fingers and loop it over the end.

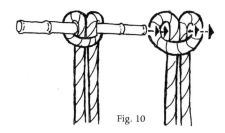

Fig. 10

Cords may also be mounted directly onto fabric or leather for fringes, tassels or other decorative trimmings (Figs. 10, 11 and 12)

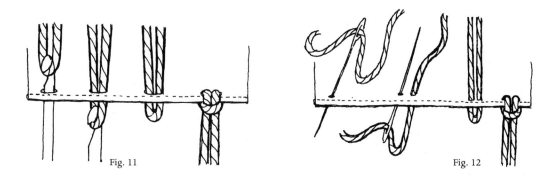

Fig. 11   Fig. 12

Even numbers of strands are commonly used for knotting, with certain exceptions, and numbers divisible by 4, 8, 12 and sometimes 16 provide the largest scope for pattern possibilities.

There are other, more elaborate ways of setting on cords. Pictures and working drawings for these can be found under 'Picots' on pages 47–50.

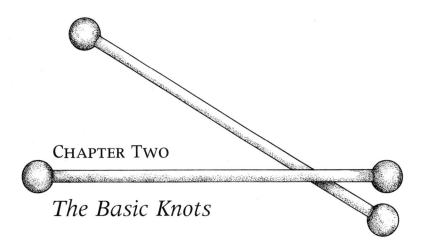

CHAPTER TWO

The Basic Knots

Macramé consists mainly of two basic knots, the **FLAT KNOT** (also called Square Knot) and the **DOUBLE HALF HITCH KNOT** (also called Clove Hitch). I find the name 'Double Half Hitch Knot' preferable because it reminds students that two movements (two Half Hitch Knots) are necessary in order to complete one secure knot.

Once these two basic knots have been mastered innumerable patterns and knot combinations are possible.

The Flat Knot

The Flat Knot is usually worked in two halves which, in order to complete one secure knot, require two cords to be pulled through in turn. When working with long strands this is not only comparatively time-consuming but can also cause excessive wear on your material. The crisp look of your knotting should be preserved as much as possible right to the end. Materials which have been handled to a great extent can look tired and grubby. Especially delicate and light-coloured yarns suffer in this way.

For these reasons I always recommend and teach the Flat Knot method which looks slightly more complicated but is quicker in the long run and preserves the neat and clean appearance of your knotting much longer. This is mainly because for each complete knot only one cord is pulled through. (Figs. 22–27.)

The Flat Knot is generally tied over four cords, two Working Cords and two Filler Cords. The Filler Cords, which are the two in the centre of the four, serve no other purpose than to 'fill' the knot, in other words act as a base for the two outside strands to work over. Keep the Filler Cords taut when knotting.

USUAL FLAT KNOT METHOD (Figs. 13–17)

Fig. 13

Fig. 14

Fig. 15

Fig. 16

Fig. 17

REVERSED FLAT KNOT (Figs. 18–21)

Fig. 18

Fig. 19

Fig. 20

Fig. 21

RECOMMENDED FLAT KNOT METHOD (Figs. 22–27)

Fig. 22

Fig. 23

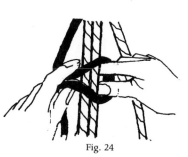
Fig. 24

Fig. 25

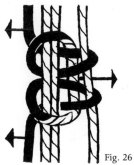
Fig. 26

Fig. 27

23

FLAT KNOT WORKED WITH TWO CORDS ONLY (Figs. 28–30)
This Flat Knot is tied in the usual way but without Filler Cords.

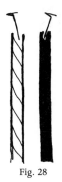

Fig. 28   Fig. 29   Fig. 30

COLLECTIVE FLAT KNOT (Fig. 31)
The Collective Flat Knot is an ordinary Flat Knot tied with one, two
or more Working Cords from either side over a multitude of Filler
Cords. An extremely attractive focal point for the centre of a
diamond shape or ring.

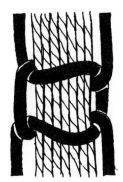

2 A variety of Alternate Flat Knot Patterns

Fig. 31

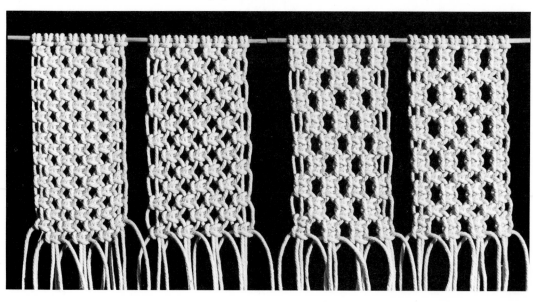

ALTERNATE FLAT KNOT PATTERN (Fig. 32)

This pattern is one of the most frequently used in Macramé work and creates a kind of fabric. Using four cords at a time, a row of Flat Knots is worked right across all strands. The number of cords must, therefore, divide by four. In the second row the first two and the last two strands remain unworked and Flat Knots are tied over all remaining cords. This produces a brickwork type of structure. Repeat the first and second rows until the required length is reached. Keep the sides straight by observing the vertical lines on the board as a guide. Along the side edges the unworked cords of the even rows should form a small loop and care must be taken not to pull the outside strands of the odd rows too tight in order not to disturb the pattern. Careful and frequent pinning will prove helpful.

A fairly dense fabric is created in this way but a more open look is possible by leaving space between each row. Work over a ruler to obtain large regular spaces.

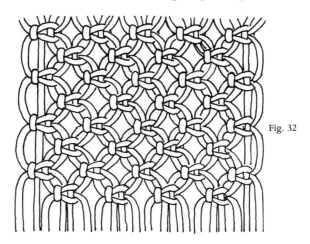

Fig. 32

ALTERNATE TWO FLAT KNOT PATTERN (Plate 2, second from right)

Work a row of two Flat Knots, one below the other, right across all strands. In the next row the first two and the last two cords stay unworked and two Flat Knots, one below the other, are tied over the remaining strands. Repeat these two rows as often as necessary.

ALTERNATE TWO AND ONE FLAT KNOT PATTERN (Plate 2, outside right)

Again two Flat Knots are tied, one below the other, right across all strands. In the next row the first two and the last two cords remain unworked and single Flat Knots are made over all other cords. Repeat these rows until the required length is reached.

TRIPLE KNOT (Figs. 33–34)

The Triple Knot consists of one complete Flat Knot and one Half Knot (top half of a Flat Knot). Rows of alternate Triple Knots slightly vary the texture produced by the Alternate Flat Knot Pattern.

Fig. 33

Fig. 34

25

BANISTER BAR (Figs. 35–36)

Difficult only in appearance, this twisted spiral can be worked in two ways, either by making continuous Half Knots (Half Flat Knots) or by tying complete Flat Knots, second version and then moving the top half in position only. There is no need to undo the second half of the knots as this will happen naturally when the next Flat Knot is worked. Knot fairly tightly in order to obtain a neat spiral and make sure your Filler Cords are kept taut. If the half knots are begun with the left-hand cord the spiral will twist to the right (Fig. 35): starting with the right-hand cord the spiral will turn to the left (Fig. 36). After completing three or four knots the spiral will begin to twist and the two Working Cords gradually reverse position (the right-hand one will be on the left and the left-hand one on the right). When this happens continue in the usual way.

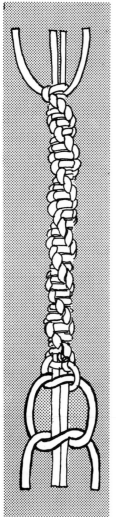

Fig. 35

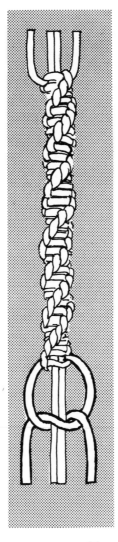

Fig. 36

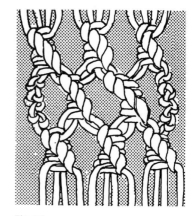

Fig. 37

26

An interesting raised texture is obtained by alternate rows of short spirals, similar in working technique to the Alternate Flat Knot Pattern. Make a row of short Banister Bars, each twisting once only. Knot a second row, leaving the first two and the last two cords unworked. Again let the Banister Bars turn once only. Repeat the first and second rows until the required length is reached (Fig. 37). The two unworked cords in the second and all even rows may be knotted with 'Single Chains' (see page 33) to give a more solid edge.

3 Wall hanging with Single and Double Crossed Knot sections, and panel with interrupted and alternated lines of Cording

SINGLE CROSSED KNOT (Figs. 38–40)
This knot is tied over four cords (two Working Cords and two Filler Cords). Tie two Half Knots (similar to Banister Bars), i.e. two top halves of a Flat Knot, then exchange the position of the Working Cords by taking the left-hand one over the Filler Cords to the right and the right-hand one under the Filler Cords to the left. For a Single Crossed Knot to face in the opposite direction the tying procedure of the Half Knots has to be reversed. Alternate rows of Single Crossed Knots give a pleasing texture (see illustration on page 27 third section from top).

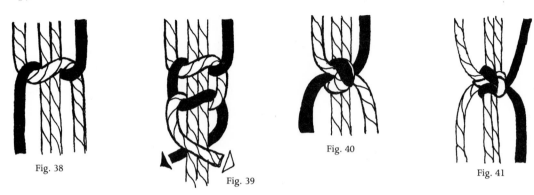

Fig. 38

Fig. 39

Fig. 40

Fig. 41

DOUBLE CROSSED KNOT (Fig. 41)
The only difference between this and the Single Crossed Knot is that three Half Knots are tied before reversing the Working Cords.

The Double Half Hitch Knot

The Double Half Hitch Knot is used to make Horizontal, Vertical or Diagonal Cording as well as for leaf shapes and covering rings, etc. Each individual knot is worked with two single cords only, one Filler Cord and one Working Cord. The Filler Cord plays a passive role and should be kept taut while the Working Cord is looped over it twice. Double Half Hitch Knots are nearly always done in multiples and arranged closely next to each other to produce a corded effect.

HORIZONTAL CORDING (Figs. 42–46)
Working from left to right:

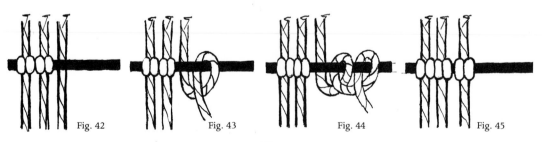

Fig. 42

Fig. 43

Fig. 44

Fig. 45

28

Working from right to left:

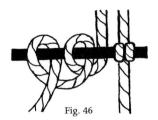

Fig. 46

To tighten a horizontal Double Half Hitch Knot it is advisable to hold the Filler Cord in a slightly upward position. This will help to keep the Cording close to the Knot Bearer or previous work. There is a tendency for beginners to knot in a downward direction which results in a sagging untidy row of Cording. Make certain that in any one row the Filler Cord and the Working Cords are not reversed. This is another beginner's favourite and results in a 'lumpy' look. As soon as this occurs undo two or three knots to find the mistake. To check that all is well it must be possible to move the Cording along the Filler Cord right across the row.

DIAGONAL CORDING (Figs. 47–50)
The process is the same as for Horizontal Cording except that the Filler Cord is at a diagonal angle. Keep all Working Cords taken into a diagonal line as straight as possible and not untidily looping over each other.

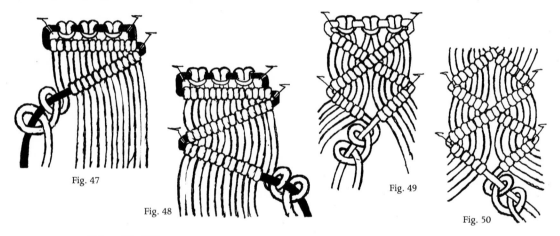

Fig. 47

Fig. 48

Fig. 49

Fig. 50

LEAF SHAPES (Figs. 51–53)
To obtain leaf shapes a more rounded line is required than a straightforward diagonal one. This is best achieved by keeping the two knots at the beginning of each leaf quite near the horizontal line immediately above and then gradually working in a downward direction. The cords from the horizontal line above taken into the top edge of each leaf should be as straight as possible and not looped or overlapping. The lower edge of the leaf should curve in the opposite way to the top. Leaves are best worked over 8 cords. Figs. 28–30 show how to work the connecting Flat Knot in fig. 53.

29

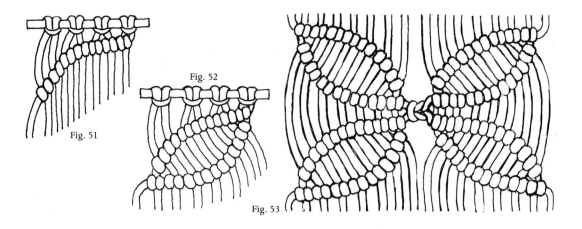

Fig. 52

Fig. 51

Fig. 53

INTERCHANGED LEAVES (Fig. 54)

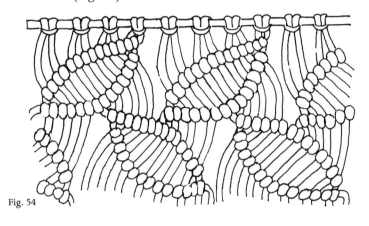

Fig. 54

OTHER EFFECTS WITH CORDING (Figs. 55–56)

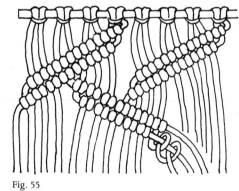

Fig. 55

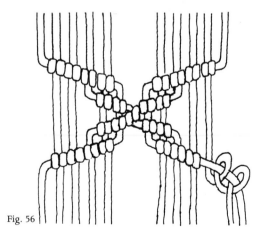

Fig. 56

VERTICAL CORDING (Figs. 57–59)

Vertical Cording differs from Horizontal Cording inasmuch as only one Working Cord is needed to be looped over any number of Filler Cords, in contrast with multiple Working Cords working over just one Filler Cord. This one Working Cord is taken back and forth making vertical Double Half Hitch Knots over all the Filler Cords, leaving small loops on both sides.

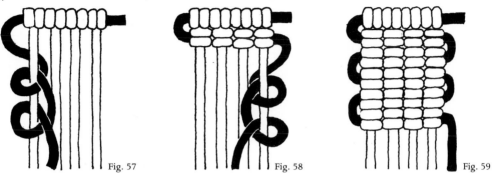

Fig. 57   Fig. 58   Fig. 59

It will help to turn the knotting board in one direction or another so that you can work towards yourself.

Half Hitch Knot (Fig. 60)

This knot is deliberately mentioned after the Double Half Hitch Knot as it is not normally worked on its own and needs a partner to form a complete and secure knot. The Half Hitch Knot is, however, very important, particularly for making Sinnets, which are described in the next chapter.

Fig. 60

Fig. 61

Buttonhole Knot (Fig. 61)

Continuous Half Hitch Knots tied with one Working Cord over one or more Filler Cords are sometimes referred to as Buttonhole Knots and can be worked from the left or from the right. If instructions tell you to make six Buttonhole Knots this means six Half Hitch Knots with the same Working Cord over one or more Filler Cords.

31

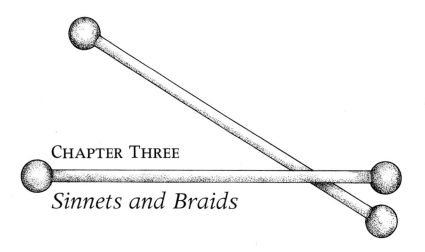

CHAPTER THREE

Sinnets and Braids

Sinnets

The term Sinnet is of nautical origin and means a single chain of knots tied continuously one below another. The effect is braid-like in contrast with patterns worked over a greater number of strands which resemble fabric.

Sinnets made up from Half Hitch Knots
1. BUTTONHOLE BAR (Figs. 62–63)
   Continuous Half Hitch Knots with one Working Cord over one or several Filler Cords, worked either from the right or from the left

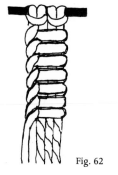

Fig. 62

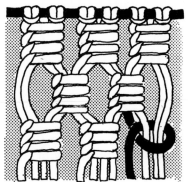

Fig. 63

Alternate short Buttonhole Bars produce an appealing fabric (Fig. 63).

32

2. CORKSCREW BAR (Fig. 64)
Worked exactly as the Buttonhole Bar but tighter which causes the edge to spiral

3. SINGLE GENOESE BAR (Fig. 65)
Worked over four cords (two Working Cords and two Filler Cords). The Working Cords in turn make a Half Hitch Knot over the two centre strands

4. GENOESE BAR (Fig. 66)
Genoese Bars can be double, treble, etc., meaning that two, three or more Half Hitch Knots are tied alternately from either the right or the left over the two Filler Cords. With groups of about seven Half Hitch Knots a waved effect is produced and Sinnets of this kind are referred to as Waved Bars

5. VARIATION ON GENOESE BAR (Fig. 67)
Worked with two Working Cords and two Filler Cords. The left-hand Working Cord makes a Half Hitch Knot over the first Filler Cord and a second Half Hitch Knot over both Filler Cords. The right-hand Working Cord then makes a Half Hitch Knot over the first Filler Cord and a second one over both Filler Cords
Each Working Cord in turn making a Half Hitch Knot over the first Filler Cord, then over both and finally over the first one only is a further possibility. The procedure is alternated from the right and then from the left

6. TATTED BAR (Fig. 68)
Tied with two Working Cords and two Filler Cords. Each Working Cord in turn makes an ordinary Half Hitch Knot and then a reversed Half Hitch Knot over the two Filler Cords. This Sinnet has looped edges and is worked alternately from the left and then the right

7. SINGLE CHAIN (Fig. 69)
Worked with two cords only. Half Hitch Knots are made in turn with the left-hand cord over the right and then with the right-hand strand over the left. The strand over which you are working must be kept taut

8. DOUBLE CHAIN (Fig. 70)
Proceed as for the Single Chain but using double cords

Sinnets made up from Flat Knots
9. FLAT KNOT SINNET (Fig. 71)
A continuous chain of Flat Knots worked one below another with two Working Cords and two Filler Cords

10. ALTERNATED FLAT KNOT SINNET (Fig. 72)
A continuous chain of Flat Knots tied alternately from the right and then from the left (usual and reversed Flat Knots)

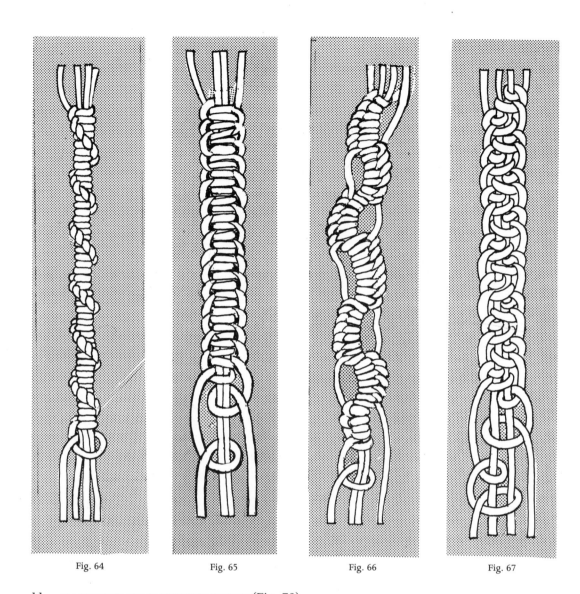

Fig. 64   Fig. 65   Fig. 66   Fig. 67

11. VARIATION ON FLAT KNOT SINNET (Fig. 73)
     Worked over four cords. The Working Cords and the Filler Cords exchange their
     function after each Flat Knot. The Filler Cords are taken from the back out to the sides
     and become Working Cords to tie a Flat Knot over the previous Working Cords which
     are now Filler Cords. Do not move the knots too closely together. The 'change over'
     should be part of the pattern

12. FLAT KNOT SINNET WITH SIDE PICOTS (Fig. 74)
     A continuous chain of Flat Knots, leaving loops at the sides formed by the Working
     Cords

34

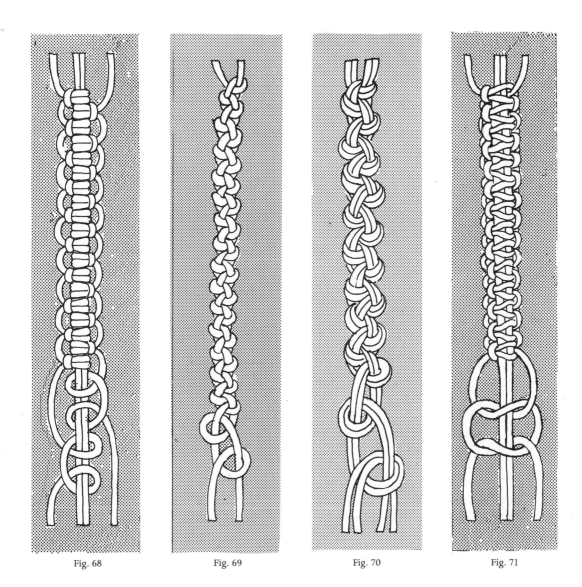

| Fig. 68 | Fig. 69 | Fig. 70 | Fig. 71 |

Overhand Knot (Figs. 75–76)

The Overhand Knot has a number of uses and may be tied with one single strand only or over several at a time. For an even appearance of a pattern this knot is sometimes worked from the left or from the right. Cord-ends can be collected and knotted off with Overhand Knots to form a kind of ornamental tassel (see Collecting and Gathering Knots on page 51).

Overhand Knots may be used to make a kind of fabric (Fig. 77).

Sinnets worked with Flat Knots and Overhand Knots

1. FLAT KNOT SINNET WITH OVERHAND KNOT SIDE PICOTS (Fig. 78)
    Tie one Flat Knot over four cords. Work an Overhand Knot on either side using each of

35

the Working Cords in turn. Continue tying Flat Knots with Overhand Knot sides.

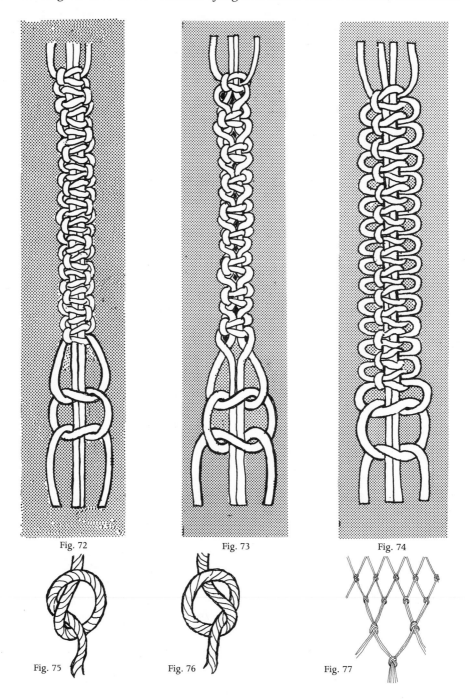

Fig. 72   Fig. 73   Fig. 74

Fig. 75   Fig. 76   Fig. 77

36

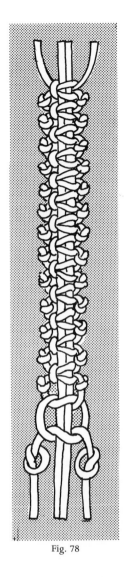

Fig. 78

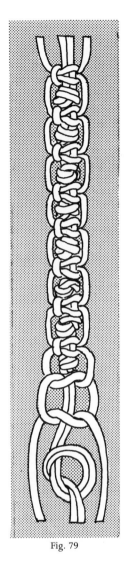

Fig. 79

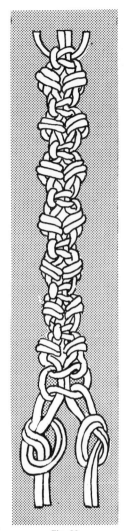

Fig. 80

2.   FLAT KNOT SINNET WITH OVERHAND KNOT CENTRE (Fig. 79)
     Tie one Flat Knot over four cords. Work an Overhand Knot with the two centre strands,
     moving it up to the Flat Knot. Continue tying Flat Knots and Overhand Knot centres
     alternately

3.   VARIATION ON FLAT KNOT SINNET WITH OVERHAND KNOTS (Fig. 80)
     Tie one Flat Knot over four cords. Curve the two left-hand strands inwards, towards the
     centre and make one Overhand Knot. Curve the two right-hand cords inwards, towards
     the centre, and make a second Overhand Knot. Continue alternating Flat Knots with two
     Overhand Knots

37

4 *A wall plaque featuring Sinnets*

5 *A selection of Macramé Braids*

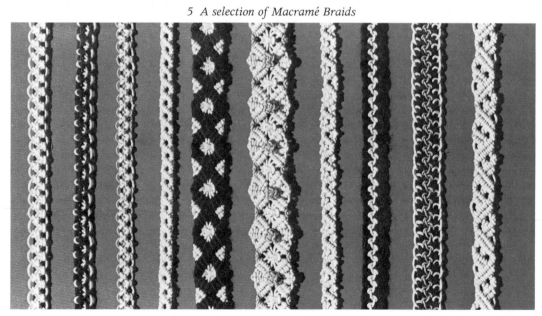

Braids (Figs. 81–82)

The basic knots and Sinnets worked in various ways and sometimes combined make it possible to produce a large variety of very attractive Braids. A selection is shown in Plate 5, some made up with two or more colours. Numbering from left to right they are as follows:

1. Alternate Flat Knot Braid (Fig. 81)
2. Alternate left and right-hand Flat Knot Braid in two colours
3. Alternate Flat Knot Braid in two colours
4. Crossed Bar (Fig. 82)
5. Braid made up from Diagonal and Vertical Cording with Flat Knot Centre
6. Braid made up from Horizontal and Vertical Cording with Flat Knot Centre in two colours
7. Braid in Diagonal Cording with Single Chain edges
8. Half Hitch Braid in two colours
9. Half Hitch Braid in three colours
10. Braid in Diagonal Cording

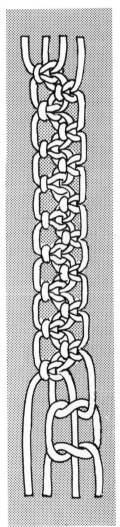

Fig. 81

Fig. 82

39

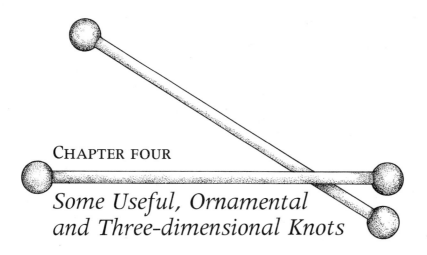

CHAPTER FOUR

Some Useful, Ornamental and Three-dimensional Knots

Useful and Ornamental Knots

Josephine Knot (Figs. 84–86)
This ornamental knot is tied with two single cords or with two sets of multiple strands. In the latter instance all cords should be kept in their proper order right through the knot. This will greatly enhance the appearance. If several Josephine Knots are worked, one below another, it is best to alternate the tying procedure, i.e. starting first from the left and then from the right. This will prevent the work from twisting. Used in belts and bags it is often desirable that Josephine Knots should be placed within diamond shapes (Fig. 83) made of Double Half Hitch Knots or other solid outlines. Pulling or weight may cause the knot to lose its attractive shape.

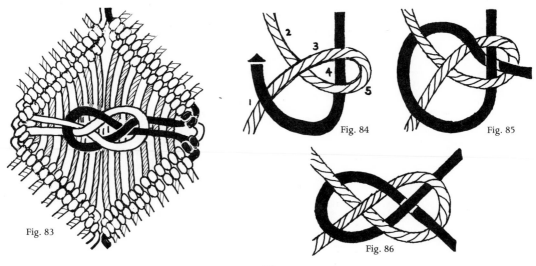

Fig. 83

Fig. 84

Fig. 85

Fig. 86

Figs. 84–86 show how to tie the Josephine Knot.

The straight cord(s) work(s) over the looped cord(s) with an over/under movement:

over 1 / under 2 / over 3 / under 4 / over 5

Straighten the knot, adjust multiple cords (if used) and gradually move in position. It is well worth spending a little time on this.

Variation resembling Josephine Knot (Figs. 87–88)
The following knot is somewhat similar to the Josephine Knot but is tied quite differently. It is worked with two or more Working Cords over two single or multiple sets of vertical strands. I am not aware of any official term for this knot but I have seen it called 'Susten-Knot', named after the Susten Pass in Switzerland with its many windings.

Fig. 87

Fig. 88

Chinese Crown Knot (Figs. 89–91)
This is another decorative knot which may be worked with two single cords or two sets of multiple strands. Unlike the Josephine Knot it never pulls out of shape once tightened. The drawings below demonstrate the tying procedure.

An interesting and very pleasing effect is achieved by using two different colours.

Fig. 89

Fig. 90

Fig. 91

Crown Knot (Figs. 92–97)
Crown Knots worked one on top of another (see drawings on the next page), result in a kind of rope. A section knotted in this way has been introduced near the top of the plant hanger shown in Colour Plate G with instructions on page 144. The weight of plant pots opens the knotting and an interesting focal point is obtained. The Crown Knot is tied with four single cords or four sets of multiple strands, coming from a collectively knotted central point. This is indicated by a circle on Figs. 92–96.

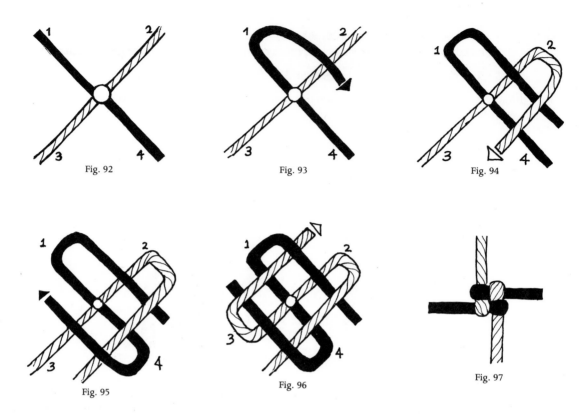

Fig. 92 Fig. 93 Fig. 94

Fig. 95 Fig. 96 Fig. 97

Triangular Knot (Figs. 98a, b)
While the Chinese Crown Knot has a square or diamond-shaped outline the Triangular Knot when tied according to the drawings below adopts the form of a triangle.

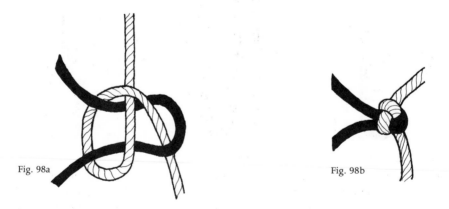

Fig. 98a Fig. 98b

Japanese Knot (Figs. 99–100)
At first sight this knot looks very involved but it basically consists of one Flat Knot tied over four cords followed by the Filler Cords being looped over the two side strands as shown in the

diagram. In the centre a Flat Knot with two Working Cords only is tied. These two strands are then again looped over the side strands. To complete make another Flat Knot over four cords. Tighten knot. The final appearance is an octagonal shape. (A group of Japanese Knots is illustrated in Plate 26 on Page 94.)

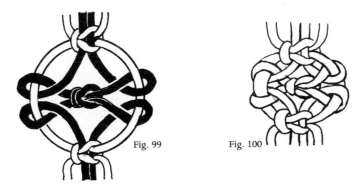

Fig. 99   Fig. 100

True Lovers' Knot (Figs. 101–103)

Perhaps not as spectacular as some the True Lovers' Knot provides an alternative for producing a fabric-like texture. It consists of two Overhand Knots, one looped through the other.

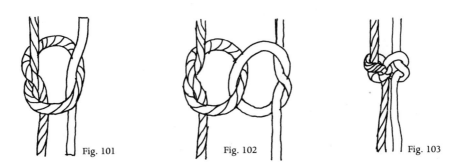

Fig. 101   Fig. 102   Fig. 103

Coil Knot (Figs. 104–105)

This knot is mainly used for decorating cord-ends. A number of Coil Knots along the base of a wall hanging or at the end of tie belts give an interesting finish and sometimes replace the use of beads.

According to the number of windings Coil Knots can be made longer or shorter.

Fig. 104   Fig. 105

43

Small Coil Knot (Figs. 106–107)
Tied as above with two windings only this knot has a crossed look on one side. Fringes with a number of horizontal rows of Small Coil Knots acquire an extremely delicate appearance (see page 27).

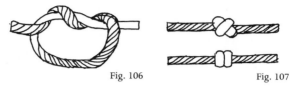

Fig. 106   Fig. 107

Three-dimensional Knots

These are made up of a number of individual knots and when worked in groups interesting raised areas emerge. Singly they are often used as a central point, e.g. where four corded lines or leaves come together, in the centre of a diamond shape, or to form lines and edges which are intended to stand out.

Bead Knot (Figs. 108–109)
The Bead Knot consists of a Sinnet of Flat Knots which is formed into a kind of loop or ball. These can be made larger or smaller as required. About four Flat Knots is the minimum for a successful Bead Knot, but this may depend on the thickness of the yarn. The two centre Filler Cords are pushed over the top of the first knot, down the back of the Sinnet and pulled tight to form a loop. The cords should be kept in their right order and the knot is completed with a Flat Knot to secure.

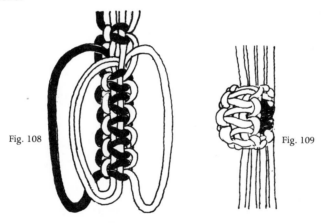

Fig. 108   Fig. 109

Note: I have found that Bead Knots are much less likely to twist or turn if the first Flat Knot is worked in such a way that two small loops are left at the top (see drawings). The centre cords are taken over the top in the ordinary way but each side cord is threaded through one of the small loops, i.e. the left-hand one through the loop on the left and the right-hand strand through the one on the right. The four cords are then pulled down the back evenly to form a Bead Knot which is held in place with another Flat Knot.

The open sides of the 'balls' often provide a useful anchorage point for beads and other trimmings (see page 148).

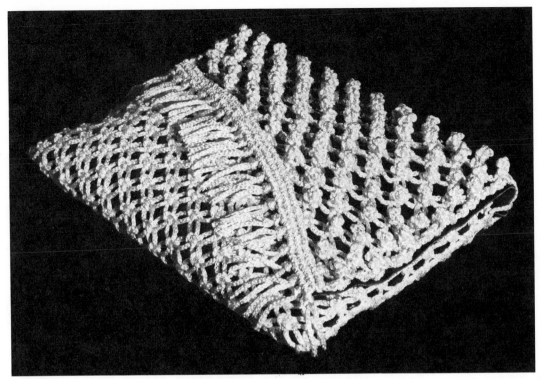

6 *Evening purse with Small Shell Knot flap*

Small Shell Knot (Figs. 110–111)
This knot begins with a Flat Knot tied over four cords, followed by a number of alternate Half Hitch Knots (Single Chain) worked with the two centre strands only, giving a longer or shorter Sinnet according to the size of knot required. The Sinnet is then pushed up to form a loop and held in place with a second Flat Knot over four cords. Grouped Small Shell Knots are used on the flap of the evening purse shown in Plate 6.

 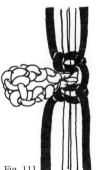  

Fig. 110   Fig. 111   Fig. 112   Fig. 113

Large Shell Knot (Figs. 112–113)
Almost identical in appearance to the Bead Knot the Shell Knot is begun in the same way by making a Flat Knot Sinnet over four cords. The two working cords are then taken up behind the Sinnet and brought to the front above the first Flat Knot. The cords must be kept in their right order. The left-hand cord and the right-hand strand are now crossed over each other immediately behind the looped Sinnet and brought out on either side. When tightening the knot the Sinnet will draw up to form a ball.

Berry Knot (Figs. 114–116)
The Berry Knot is a combination of Flat Knots and Double Half Hitch Knots. The simplest form resembles a Raspberry or Blackberry (Plate 7). There are variations which are obtained by combining Horizontal and Vertical Cording in the 'berry' part of the knot. A raised effect is produced and quite impressive patterns can be worked. The Cording can be made to slope either from right to left or left to right.

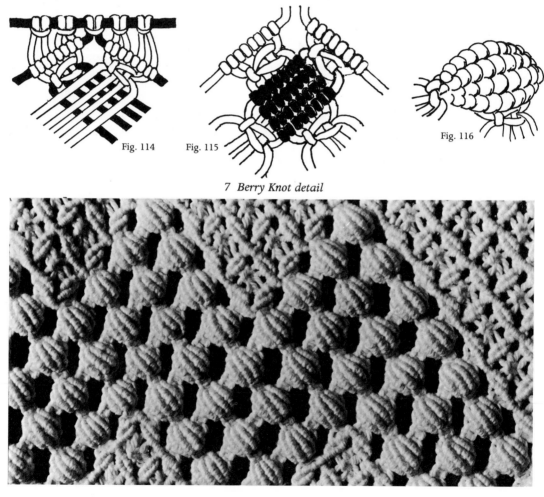

Fig. 114   Fig. 115   Fig. 116

7 Berry Knot detail

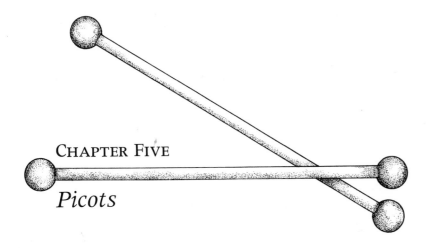

CHAPTER FIVE

Picots

Picots, as shown in Plate 8 on page 50, are ornamental headings. They are prettier and more elaborate beginnings to work than the ordinary Lark's Head Knots and very decorative on lampshades, wall hangings or evening bags. With a little experimentation it is possible to make up a much larger number of different kinds than is normally shown in books. The selection illustrated includes some more unusual ones.

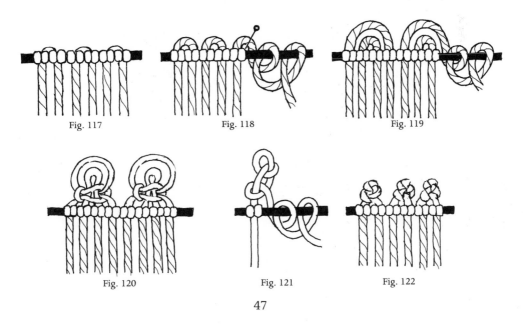

Fig. 117   Fig. 118   Fig. 119

Fig. 120   Fig. 121   Fig. 122

Fig. 123

Fig. 124

Fig. 125

Fig. 126

Fig. 127

Fig. 128

Fig. 129

Fig. 130

Fig. 131

Fig. 132

Fig. 133

Fig. 134

Fig. 135

Fig. 136

Fig. 137

48

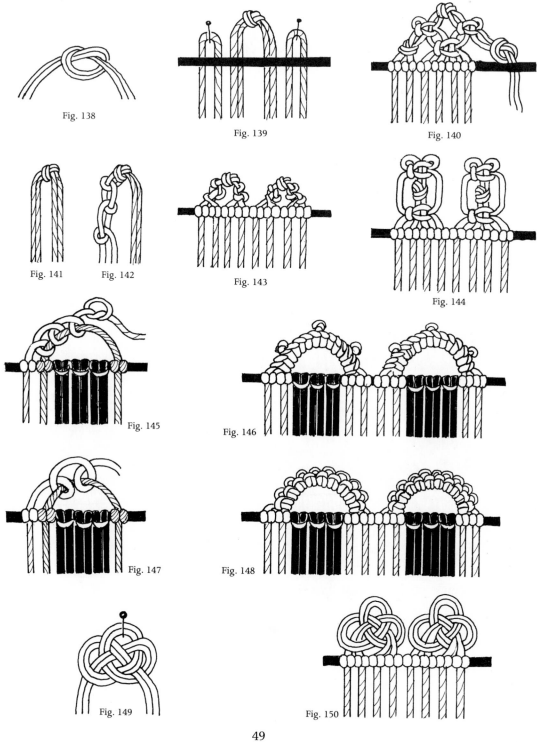

Fig. 138

Fig. 139

Fig. 140

Fig. 141   Fig. 142

Fig. 143

Fig. 144

Fig. 145

Fig. 146

Fig. 147

Fig. 148

Fig. 149

Fig. 150

49

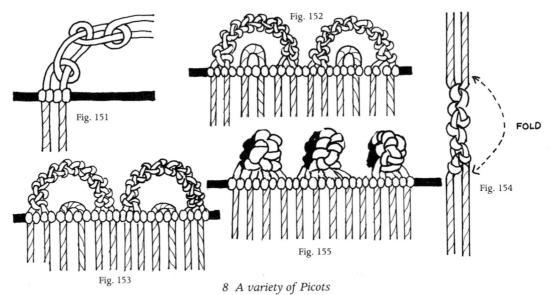

Fig. 151

Fig. 152

Fig. 153

Fig. 154

Fig. 155

FOLD

8 A variety of Picots

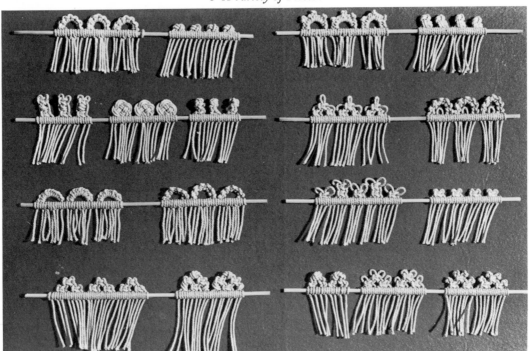

Picots are also a way of hiding knot bearers completely, unlike Lark's Head Knots which only cover at intervals. This is an advantage when the knot bearer is either not very interesting or unsightly. The simplest form of Picot, when tightened so that the little loop at the top does not show (Fig. 117) makes a perfect corded line when several are tied in a row.

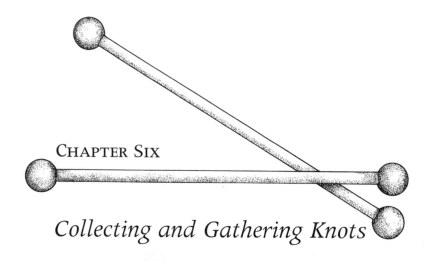

CHAPTER SIX

Collecting and Gathering Knots

Overhand Knot as Collecting Knot (Fig. 156)
An Overhand Knot (see Overhand Knot on page 35) may be used for gathering numbers of cord-ends together. Done collectively on a large group of strands this knot may, however, become too bulky and other methods prove more successful, unless one or two strands only are used to make an Overhand Knot over the remaining cords. This form of Overhand Knot is known as a Marling Knot.

 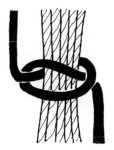  

Fig. 156   Fig. 157   Fig. 158

Fig. 159

Marling Knot (Fig. 157)

Collecting Knot (Fig. 158)
One or two strands from the right-hand side of a group of cords to be gathered are used. Make a loop as shown in the drawing, bring the cord(s) round the front and then the back of the group, through the loop and tighten. A more solid looking tassel is obtained if several of these

knots are worked closely one below another. The gathering cord may be looped over the wrappings at the back of work and brought down again by pushing the end through on the inside with a needle. Fig. 159 shows a row of tassels tied with Collecting Knots.

Constrictor Knot (Figs. 160–162)
This is another Collecting Knot, slightly more complicated and is tied round a number of cords with a separate piece of yarn.

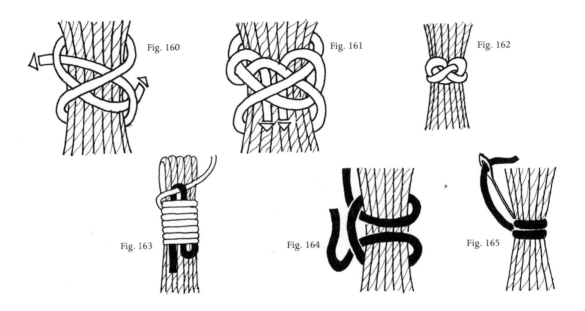

Fig. 160 Fig. 161 Fig. 162

Fig. 163 Fig. 164 Fig. 165

Wrapping Cord (Fig. 163)
A separate wrapping cord may be used for wrapping round a number of strands. Make a loop with one end of this cord. Place it on top of the strands to be gathered and hold firmly in position. Start wrapping over all cords and the loop end, working from the bottom upwards. When the required number of wrappings is completed put the end of the gathering cord through the top of the loop. Pull loop end down until the wrapping end is inside the coil then cut off ends. To make it more secure a small amount of fabric glue may be put onto the loop of the wrapping cord before it is pulled down. This technique is sometimes known as whipping.

For wrapping the ends of a Plant Hanger to form a tassel see page 144.

Alternative Collecting Knot (Figs. 164–165)
The small tassels on the lantern shown in Colour Plate A have been gathered by using a cord from the outside left of each group to make one Half Hitch Knot and an inverted Half Hitch Knot over the strands to be collected. The end of the Working Cord was then taken up on the reverse side of the two Half Hitch Knots and pushed down the centre with a needle to become part of the tassel ends.

52

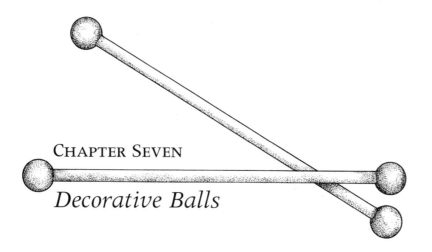

CHAPTER SEVEN

Decorative Balls

Monkey's Fist (Figs. 166–171)

Sailors work large versions of this ball-shaped knot over heavy stones in order to make weights for anchoring their dinghies to the beach. In Macramé this ball is intended for decorative purposes on hangings, lampshades, belt ends, etc. But also for buttons with a loop for fastening. According to the thickness of the yarn and the size ball required a cord of about $1\frac{1}{2}$ to 2 yards (1.34–1.82 m) or more is necessary.

Wind four times vertically over index and middle finger, holding the beginning of the cord in place with your thumb.

Bring the cord between the two fingers and wrap from the back four times horizontally around all strands. Start winding from the bottom upwards and not too tightly.

Bring the cord to the front of the horizontal wrapping, through the top loop and then the bottom loop. Wind through these loops four times.

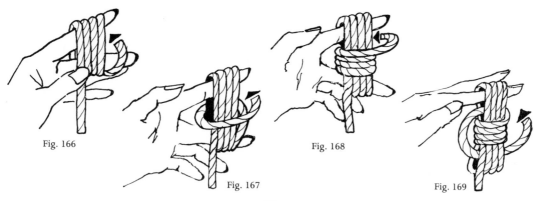

Fig. 166

Fig. 167

Fig. 168

Fig. 169

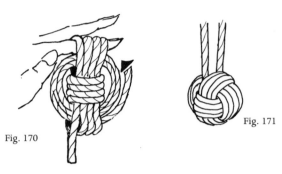

Fig. 170

Fig. 171

Insert a suitable-sized bead into the centre. Push end of cord through bottom loop.

Now tighten cord, starting at one end and following through right round the bead. Make sure the strands lie neatly next to each other in their proper order. The sorting out of the ball takes a little time.

Turk's Head (Figs 172–174)
This is another sailor's knot which can be worked flat and then formed into a ball. The length of the Working Cord depends on the thickness of the yarn and the size knot required.

Fig. 172    Fig. 173    Fig. 174

TO MAKE SAMPLE
Fold the cord in half and pin the loop to the board. With the two cord-ends make a Josephine Knot (see 'Josephine Knot' on page 40).

Take the right cord-end and follow through the circuit of the left strand until the pattern is completely double.

TO MAKE A BALL
Gradually tighten the loops to form a rounded shape (insert a bead if wished). This ball is again suitable for ornamental purposes or buttons.

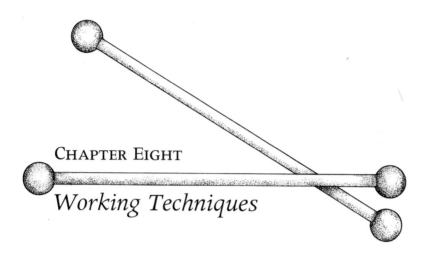

CHAPTER EIGHT

Working Techniques

Working to a point

To work a point at the end of a belt, on handbag flaps, or at the base of a wall hanging is not as difficult as it may seem. All patterns providing diagonal lines can be brought to a natural point by gradually leaving out cords on both sides. The following drawings demonstrate various methods.

9a–b Thick wool shawl worked to a point

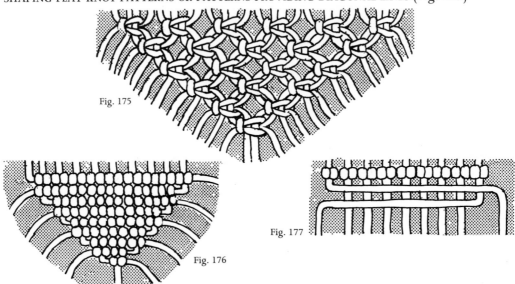

Fig. 175

Fig. 176

Fig. 177

SHAPING HORIZONTAL CORDING (Figs. 176–177)

The cord-ends can either be sewn in the back or knotted off at the sides with an Overhand Knot and left hanging down.

Placing one cord from either side over and against each other to form a double Filler Cord, the ends of which are left out in each row, is a further possibility for shaping. In some instances this might, however, make the work too bulky.

It is often desirable when knotting is worked to a point that the edges at the end should consist of several rows of Cording. This provides an excellent base on which to glue cord-ends at the back of work, thereby concealing these (see Fig. 276 on page 105).

The point depends on the number of cords. The larger the number the bigger the point.

Working from a point (Figs. 178–181)

The techniques shown below are not only used when starting work from a point, but may also serve as a means of adding new cords in order to increase the pattern area. This is often desirable on belts and bags when the buckles or handles do not allow for the sufficient mounting of cords to make the work look in proportion (see 'Hints on making up practical pieces of work' on page 104).

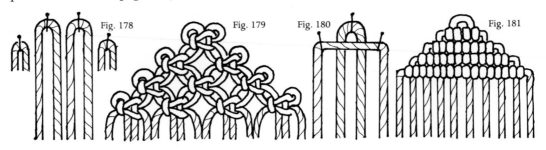

Fig. 178   Fig. 179   Fig. 180   Fig. 181

Zig-zags are obtained by using either Horizontal or Vertical Cording or a combination of both which is known as the **Angling Technique**. Two sections of Zig-zags worked next to each other and in opposite directions can be intertwined as shown in Fig. 185.

TO MAKE ZIG-ZAGS WITH HORIZONTAL CORDING (Figs. 182–184)

Plate 10 shows a wall hanging featuring this technique. Set a number of cords onto a Holding Cord or other Knot Bearer (about 2 to 3, giving 4 to 6 Working Cords). Secure the right-hand strand of this group with a pin and place it horizontally over all remaining strands as Filler Cord. Make a row of Horizontal Cording over it with each cord in turn, starting from the right. (Fig. 182)* Now bring the next strand on the right round a pin and place it from right to left horizontally over all remaining cords. Using each strand in turn work a row of Horizontal Cording over it, starting from the right, including the previous Filler Cord at the end. Repeat from * twice more.

You should now have four rows of Horizontal Cording sloping from right to left. Bring the last Filler Cord on the left round a pin and place it horizontally across all remaining strands from left to right. Knot a row of Horizontal Cording over it with each strand in turn, starting from the left (Fig. 183).

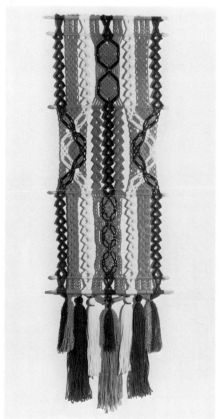

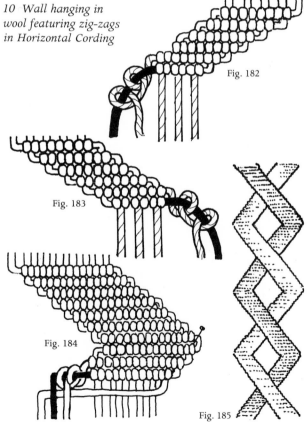

10 Wall hanging in wool featuring zig-zags in Horizontal Cording

Fig. 182

Fig. 183

Fig. 184

Fig. 185

**Using the next cord on the left, bring it round a pin and horizontally over all remaining strands on the right. Make a row of Horizontal Cording over it with each strand in turn, starting from the left, including the last Filler Cord on the right. Starting from ** work a further six rows of Cording. This section should slope from left to right. To bring work back again reverse the last Filler Cord on the right round a pin and place it horizontally over all remaining strands on the left (Fig. 184). Make eight rows of Cording sloping from right to left as worked in the first section. Continue reversing direction after every eighth row until required length is reached.

To intertwine (Fig. 185) make a second zig-zag section by mounting the same number of cords to the right of the already set on strands and knot the zig-zags in the opposite way. For wider zig-zags set on more cords and increase the number of rows of Cording between corners to obtain neat overlapping.

TO MAKE ZIG-ZAGS WITH VERTICAL CORDING (Figs. 186–187)
Plate 11 shows a hanging featuring this technique. The process is similar to that for Horizontal Cording. Mount two or three cords onto a Knot Bearer (giving 4 to 6 Working Cords). Using the strand on the outside right of the group as Working Cord, bring it round a pin and make a row of Vertical Cording over all strands, starting from the right (Fig. 187).* Bring the next strand on the right round a pin as Working Cord and knot another row of Vertical Cording over all remaining strands, starting from the right and including the previous Working cord at the end. Repeat from * twice more.

You should now have four rows of Vertical Cording sloping from right to left. Bring the last Working Cord on the outside left round a pin and make a row of Vertical Cording over all remaining strands, starting from the left (Fig. 186).

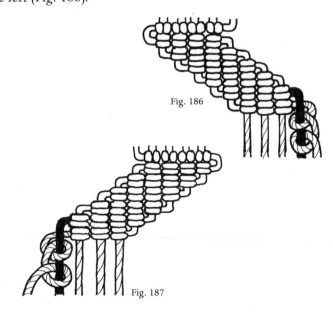

Fig. 186

Fig. 187

11 Wall hanging in jute illustrating vertically corded Zig-zags

58

Use the next cord on the left as Working Cord, bring it round a pin and work another row of Vertical Cording over the remaining strands, including the previous Working Cord at the end. Starting from ** make six more rows of Vertical Cording in the same manner. To bring work back again to the left, use the last Working Cord on the outside right, bring it round a pin and work a row of Vertical Cording over all remaining strands, starting from the right. ***Take the next cord on the right as Working Cord and make a row of Vertical Cording over all remaining strands, starting from the right and including the last Working Cord. Repeat from * six more times. Continue alternating direction until the work has reached the required length.

To intertwine mount a second group of cords (same number as before) to the right of the completed section and work zig-zags in the opposite direction. For wider zig-zags mount more cords and increase the number of rows between corners to obtain neat overlapping.

Angling technique (Figs. 188–189)
This technique consists of areas knotted alternately in either Horizontal or Vertical Cording to give corners and shaped sections. If worked in two colours, each one will show in turn according to the direction and type of Cording used. Figs. 188 and 189 show the basic technique. A very attractive example of knotting continuous corners is illustrated on page 156 in the shape of a bellpull.

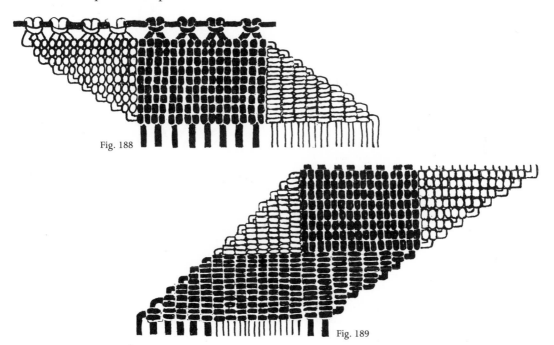

Fig. 188

Fig. 189

Knotting from the centre
1. IN TWO DIRECTIONS (Figs. 190–191)
To avoid working with very long cords some students prefer to start items like belts or table mats in the centre, knotting first in one direction and then in the other. This is very tempting

59

but it must be remembered that any Flat Knots included in the pattern have to be reversed when working the second half. Failing this the knots look upside down and this is particularly noticeable with large Collective Flat Knots. Purely corded patterns can be knotted in both directions without the fabric changing in appearance.

Cording Method: To start Cording in the centre all strands are cut to half the normally required length as they will be mounted singly and are not folded in half. At the midway point place the cord on the outside left as Holding Cord at right angles across all Working Cords. Pin each single strand above this Holding Cord and use each cord in turn to make a Double Half Hitch Knot over it from below. Work may now progress in one direction and then the other until the required length is reached.

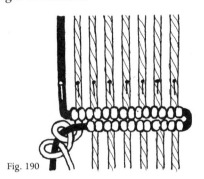

Fig. 190

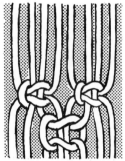

Fig. 191

Flat Knot Method: Again all cords are mounted singly and have to be cut to half the normally required length. For a Flat Knot Pattern simply make a row of Flat Knots halfway along the cut cords then knot the first half. For the above-stated reason remember to reverse all Flat Knots when working the second half.

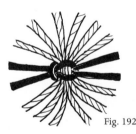

Fig. 192

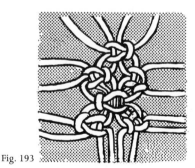

Fig. 193

2. IN A CIRCULAR FASHION (Figs. 192–200)

Certain items like circular mats, some plant hangers, certain lampshades, etc. are to best advantage knotted in the round, starting work in the centre. The following drawings show various ways in which this can be done.

(a) Making a Collective Flat Knot over a number of Filler Cords, then spacing out all strands in a circular fashion (Figs. 192–193)
(b) Collecting a number of cords with an Overhand Knot and spacing out all strands in a circular pattern (Figs. 194–195)

(c) Setting strands onto a circular holding cord or directly onto a plastic or wooden ring (Fig. 196)

(d) Making a Collective Flat Knot over a number of Filler Cords and mounting the ends onto a ring or separate holding cord (Fig. 197)

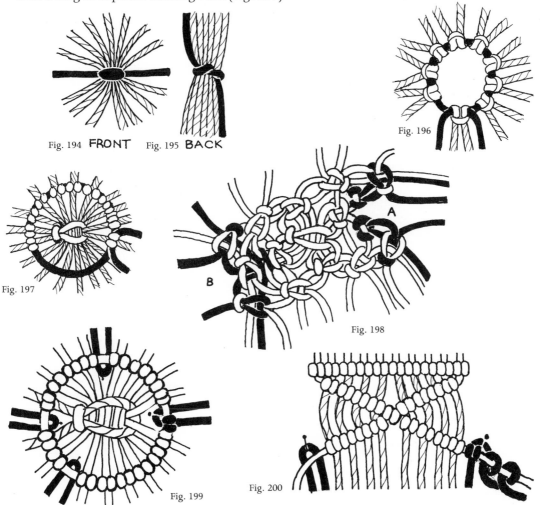

Fig. 194 FRONT Fig. 195 BACK

Fig. 196

Fig. 197

Fig. 198

Fig. 199

Fig. 200

In circular knotting, unless work is gradually opened out, new cords will have to be added as required in order to obtain a denser fabric. Choosing the most suitable places to do this is, on the whole, best left to the knotter's judgment and may vary from item to item. Figs. 198–200 show various possibilities:

   (a) New cords brought into work with inverted Lark's Head Knots (A) and additional cords looped over existing work then forming Flat Knots (B) (Fig. 198)
   (b) Extra cords added along a circle (Fig. 199)
   (c) New cords joined in along diagonally corded lines (Fig. 200)

61

3. FROM A SQUARE (IN FOUR DIRECTIONS) (Figs. 201–207)

METHOD 1: Position four cords to form a square as shown in Fig. 201. First link cord A and cord B together by working a Double Half Hitch Knot with cord B over cord A. Next set one or two strands onto cord A by pushing the loops of the folded cords under it, securing these with pins, and making one Double Half Hitch Knot over cord A with each cord-end in turn. Move these knots close to the linked strands A and B. Now make one Double Half Hitch Knot with cord A over cord C. Mount one or two doubled strands onto cord B as before. Tie one Double Half Hitch Knot with cord D over cord B. Set a further one or two doubled strands onto cord D as before. Work one Double Half Hitch Knot with cord C over cord D to join. Finally mount one or two more doubled strands onto cord C to complete the square.

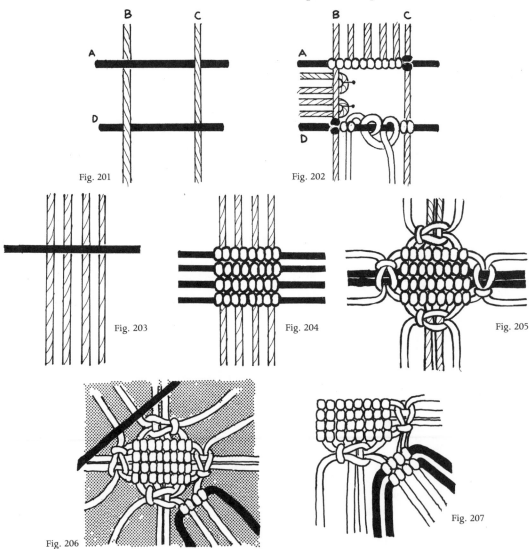

Fig. 201

Fig. 202

Fig. 203

Fig. 204

Fig. 205

Fig. 206

Fig. 207

METHOD 2: Form a square by vertically aligning four cords and, in turn, placing four further strands over these at right angles, making Double Half Hitch Knots over each one with the ends from the four vertical strands (Figs. 203 and 204).
Knotting may now proceed in all four directions (Fig. 205). Cords can be added at the corners with inverted Lark's Head Knots or using one of the methods shown in Figs. 206–207.

Joining cords (Figs. 208–211)
Although it would be ideal not to have to join cords at all, this sometimes becomes necessary and even most experienced knotters are not immune to this. In the case of a random pattern or very close work it is impossible to know in advance which cords will run short. You are, therefore, well advised to be overgenerous when cutting yarn. Having to join in many strands is very tedious work and the joins are not always easily disguised.

Some ways of adding new cords to obtain a widening fabric are shown under 'Working from a point' on page 56 and 'Knotting from the centre' on page 61. The drawings below demonstrate methods of actual replacement of strands once they have become too short. With some experience the knotter will, in time, find ways of doing this in the least obvious fashion.
1. *Splicing*: Splicing (Figs. 208 and 209) is in certain circumstances the only successful method for joining thick yarns, the 'lumpy' effect created by a double thickness of yarn becoming immediately noticeable. Untwist the end of the old cord for about one or two inches ($2\frac{1}{2}$–5 cm) and cut away half the individual strands. Prepare one end of the new cord in a similar way. Dab a very small amount of fabric glue onto both prepared ends and twist these together to make up the original thickness of the yarn. Joins of this kind are not obvious when using the 'fluffier' kind of materials like jute and sisal. Splicing is beautifully concealed when Cording is worked over it or when the splice is taken into a Sinnet as a Filler Cord. Depending on the pattern a thick strand can be joined in successfully between two rows of Cording (see part 4 of this section). The ends may need unravelling and the individual strands are then sewn into the back of work.

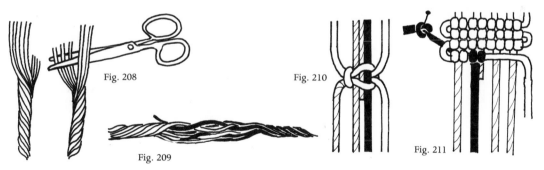

Fig. 208

Fig. 209

Fig. 210

Fig. 211

2. Thinner yarns do not, as a rule, need splicing. In a Flat Knot Pattern join the new strands, if possible, at a point when the short cord is a Filler Cord (Fig. 210). The new thread is inserted in the centre as an additional Filler Cord and the Flat Knot tied slightly tighter than usual to counteract the extra bulk created by the treble Filler Cords. The end of the old cord and the beginning of the new one are eventually sewn in the back of work. If a new strand is added in this way and several Flat Knots are knotted over it, as for example in a Sinnet, there is no need to sew the ends in. They are simply cut off.

3. In Cording the beginning of the new cord may be placed on top of the short one to give a double Filler Cord over which Double Half Hitch Knots are tied, tightening these rather more than usual to reduce the bulk. If this method makes the join too obvious use Splicing as described above.

4. Joining in new Working Strands in a corded pattern is best done by taking these straight into the work. Make an Overhand Knot at one end of the new cord and pin this to the board several inches (about 12 cm) above the point where it is to be joined in. Take the strand down the back of work and bring it out to the front in the appropriate place to make a Double Half Hitch Knot over the Filler Cord. Push the old strand to the back and eventually sew both ends in on the reverse side after untying the Overhand Knot in the new strand.

5. Sometimes it is possible to reverse the function of cords when it becomes obvious that certain strands are running short as described under 'Useful tips' 3. on page 120.

Joining sections together (Figs. 212–215)
Two or more sections often require joining together, particularly for bags of all kinds. This can be done either by knotting or sewing. There are no hard and fast rules as to when sections should either be knotted or sewn together. Always use the method which looks most successful. Neat joins are more easily achieved if some advance thought is given to the edges of the work. Corded edges are difficult to join unless small loops are left where the Filler Cords are reversed. The Alternate Flat Knot Pattern provides natural loops and presents no problems. Pieces with long unworked side cords or long side Sinnets are not very suitable and it is best to calculate your pattern in such a way that any loose strands or Sinnets should fall into the main centre area and not along the side edges.

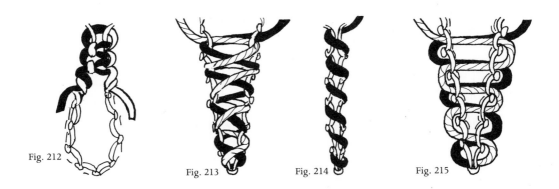

Fig. 212   Fig. 213   Fig. 214   Fig. 215

Figs. 212–215 show various ways of joining sections together either by knotting or sewing.
1.   Knotting together by using a Flat Knot worked with two cords (Using a double strand, a Flat Knot over four cords could be tied)
2.   Sewing together by putting cords through the side loops, crossing these over each other before pushing the ends through the next set of loops
3.   Oversewing through loops
4.   Joining with running stitches through the side loops, first in one direction and then the other

Edges

Macramé work is greatly enhanced if particular attention is paid to neat and sometimes decorative edges (see also 'Joining sections together' on page 64. Cording produces strong edges and is used to give a frame-like appearance to squares and rectangles.

PICOTS OVER THE EDGE (Figs. 216–217)

These are very decorative on braids, table mats, handbag flaps, etc. The two outside cords are left straight and unworked while the next two or more strands are worked in such a way that at certain points they are knotted over the side cords with vertical Double Half Hitch Knots. A Picot is then formed and the cords are brought back into the main pattern area after making vertical Double Half Hitch Knots over the side strands again. The working procedure for two side Picots is shown in Figs. 216 and 217.

Fig. 216

Fig. 217

12 Shoulder bag in cotton twine with Picots worked over the side edges of the flap

65

In the case of a firescreen, magazine rack, flower trough or any item where the knotting is done within a frame, the vertical outside cords are replaced by the sides or side rods over which the Cording is done instead. Because of the firmness of a metal or wooden rod one vertically corded row is quite sufficient (see also 'Firescreens, magazine racks, flower troughs, etc.' on page 117. A flower trough is shown in Colour Plate A.

How to insert a ring (Figs. 218–219)
The hanging in Plate 13 incorporates several ovals and a ring. To make circles and ovals in Macramé work a solid base is required for knotting over. Rings ranging from the smallest curtain ring to bangles and large circles and ovals made from basket cane may serve this purpose. Whatever the nature of the base the method of insertion remains the same. The only thing that varies is the number of cords which is, of course, determined by the size of ring and the thickness of the yarn used for covering. Begin at the top, in the centre, work Double Half Hitch Knots alternately down both sides, keeping the ring in its proper place. When half the circle is covered the same cords will be used again for filling in the lower portion. The halfway mark is, therefore, the guide to how many cords will be required to cover the whole ring. Push all cords to the back before working the second half. A needle is sometimes necessary to thread the last strand over the ring and through the loops.

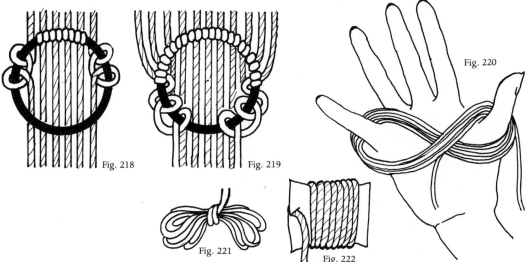

Fig. 218

Fig. 219

Fig. 220

Fig. 221

Fig. 222

Tying long cords into bundles (Figs. 220–222)
Most books recommend tying long cord-ends into bundles to make them more manageable and to keep them in order. This is a subject I should preferably like to avoid because it defeats me! However long my Working Cords I always leave them loose. When knotting a pattern cords are rarely used in strict sequence. It is, therefore, necessary to sort out the right bundle each time. These have a habit of tangling and becoming looped around each other. On occasions, students having read a book at home, appear in class proudly displaying their many neatly tied and rubber-banded bundles. When I am asked to give help with such a piece of work a feeling of total frustration comes over me and my first move is to release at least some of the carefully prepared strands. Having made this admission—how do I cope?

13 Wall hanging in fine rayon yarn demonstrating the introduction of rings and ovals

First of all I put all cords which are not part of the section I am working on out of the way. Secondly I rather spread myself inasmuch as I throw the cords which I have just used out to the side. It is a good idea, whenever possible, to start knotting from one side and in the next row from the other. On turning back, each time, the strands required first were knotted last in the previous row. Therefore, they lie uppermost or certainly not very far down and can easily be separated from the rest with a slight shaking action. Always put the cords with which you have finished for the moment out of the way: to the left when working from left to right and to the right when knotting from right to left. The only time when I may have to sort out a tangle is with long, and at the same time very thin, yarns. However, I much prefer sorting out a tangle once in a while to coping with lots of bundles all the time. One instance when bundles are an advantage is when knotting long Sinnets. Tying the Working Cords speeds up the process. Should you be looking for the challenge of working with bundles successfully, you could try the Butterfly method (Figs. 220 and 221) or the Bobbin method (Fig. 222).

14 Samples of knotted tassels

Plain and Patterned tassels (Figs. 223–226)
Collecting numbers of cords with either Overhand Knots or one of the Gathering Knots is described under 'Collecting and Gathering Knots' on page 51. Larger and more decorative tassels are obtained by dividing the cord-ends of a completed project into groups. The cords of these groups are then halved and the two sets of strands looped over each other in a similar way to the first action of tying a shoe lace. Numbers of new cords are then cut to make up the desired thickness of the tassels, placing these over the 'shoe-lace knot'. All strands are then collected with either a separate wrapping cord (see 'Collecting and Gathering Knots' on page

51) or a small metal or wooden ring which is slipped over the cord-ends. The ring may first be covered with yarn using Half Hitch Knots. Sinnets formed into small circles and passed into position over the cord-ends are most effective.

Tassels may, of course, also be worked separately and are then sewn or tied onto a particular piece of work with the help of a cord which is threaded through the loops at the top of the tassel head. Tassel heads can be made more elaborate by knotting the outermost cords with a Macramé pattern. Such tassels are particularly attractive at the end of curtain cords or light pulls, etc.

The hanging cord for decorative tassels could consist of a long knotted Chain, Sinnet or Twisted Cord.

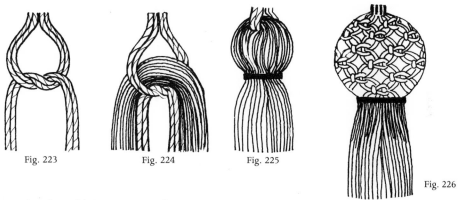

Fig. 223   Fig. 224   Fig. 225

Fig. 226

Making a twisted cord (Figs. 227–229)
Most of us have at some time or another made twisted cords for drawstrings, etc. The instructions below are for readers who have not had cause to do this.

The number of strands depends on the thickness of yarn used and the size of cord required. To make a sample (Figs. 227–229) use a piece of ordinary parcel twine or wool about $2\frac{1}{2}$ yards (2.30 m) long. Fold this in half and tie the ends together with an Overhand Knot (see page 35).

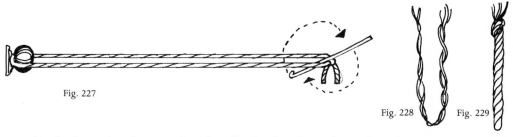

Fig. 227

Fig. 228   Fig. 229

Now slip the looped end over a door handle, hook or key of a cupboard, etc. Insert a knitting needle, small stick or a pen between the two strands at the Overhand Knot end. Keeping the cords taut hold these lightly with your left hand, just behind the inserted object. Turn the knitting needle or stick round and round with the index finger of your right hand until a fairly tight twisted cord is obtained. With your left hand hold the centre of this cord and keeping it stretched all the time bring the two ends together. Remove the cord from the door handle, etc., hold ends firmly and slowly release the left hand. The doubled strands should now naturally wind themselves round each other to form a ropelike twisted cord. Tie an Overhand Knot over all four strands on the open-ended side to prevent untwisting.

Using medium thick parcel twine this cord should now be about 12 in (30 cm) long. Making a sample will serve as a guide for lengths of cords to be cut.

How to work in sections (Figs. 230–233)

Some of my work is made up in individual sections, particularly wall hangings knotted with very fine yarn. This is partly done to preserve the new look of the material but also because the fringed divisions between patterns are unusual and very attractive. New cords are used either for each section or every second, third, etc. (see Plates 15a–k on pages 70–72).

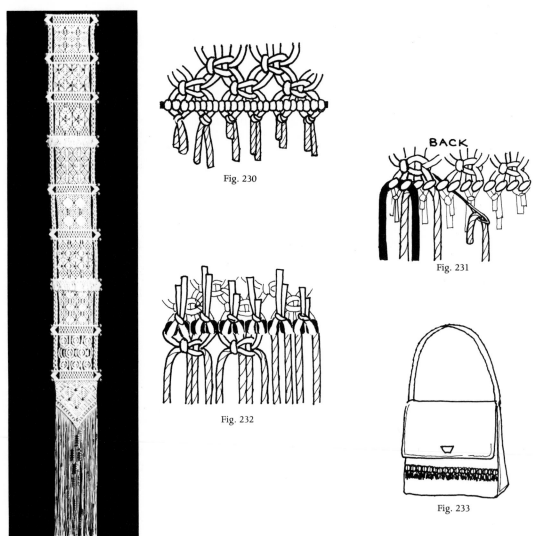

Fig. 230

BACK

Fig. 231

Fig. 232

Fig. 233

15a Heirloom wall panel in nylon fishing twine knotted in sections

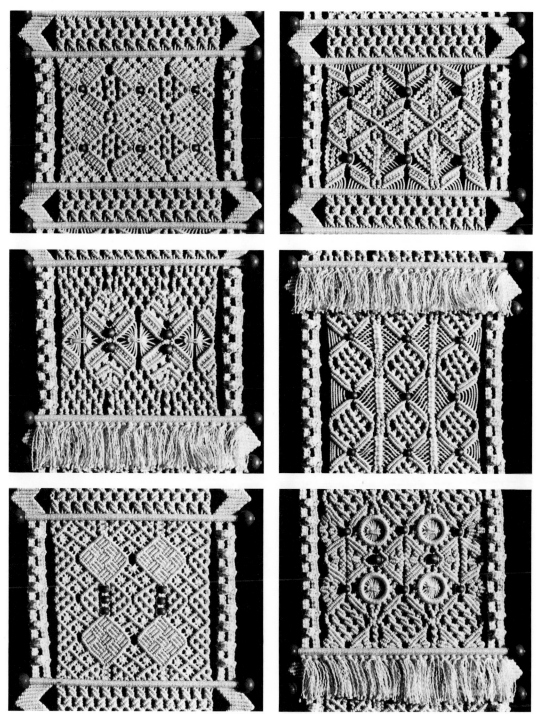

15b–g Details of wall panel

15h–k Details of wall panel

72

Cut your cords long enough to make as many pattern sections as required, then end the knotting with a row of Horizontal Cording (this may be worked over a wooden support as is used in the hanging, Plates 15a–k). Using two cords at a time knot off all strands with Overhand Knots. Do not trim the fringe immediately. Cut new cords, the same number as before and most likely the same length unless for some reason you require a longer or shorter distance between the fringes. Turn the work over onto the reverse side and using a needle thread the new strands in turn through the small loops formed at the back of the corded line, catching two of these at a time (Figs. 230–231). Pull all ends even. You should now have the same number of Working Cords as before. Turn the knotting back, right side up, and pin it to the board. Push the fringe out of the way (Fig. 232) (cut fringes interfere at this stage as they cannot be moved up). Tie a few rows of Alternate Flat Knots or any suitable pattern to form a dividing line between the two sections. End with a second row of Horizontal Cording, again worked over a support, if used. You are now ready to knot your next pattern area.

Repeat this process as many times as necessary until the project has reached the desired length. Cut the fringes just below the lower corded line of the divisions and in the beginning preferably slightly longer. Knotted pieces sometimes stretch a little when hung up with the danger of the fringes eventually not covering the entire dividing line. While a fraction more can be cut off later, there is no way of lengthening the strands once trimmed.

With some thought this method can sometimes be used when cords have been cut too short. A beaded fringe on a handbag for example, followed by more knotting, looks very exclusive and an accident can be turned into an individual creation (Fig. 233).

Detail of wall hanging in jute. Plate 11 page 58

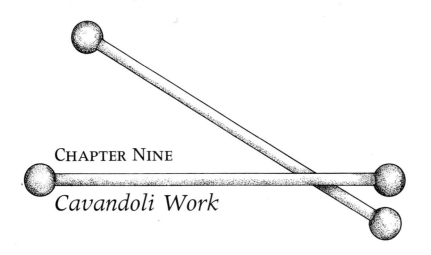

CHAPTER NINE

Cavandoli Work

This technique was used at the beginning of this century by Mrs. Valentina Cavandoli to occupy young children at an open air school in Turin, Italy. It consists of a combination of Horizontal and Vertical Cording and is knotted in two colours. The background is worked in one colour with Horizontal Cording and the design in another with Vertical Cording. Any cross stitch pattern provides a design for Cavandoli Work. According to the type of yarn used the effect becomes virtually tapestry-like and a very solid, durable fabric is produced.

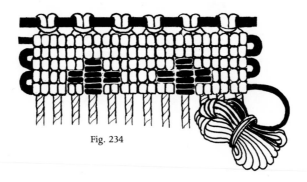

Fig. 234

Mount the required number of cords with the background colour. The contrasting yarn remains in a ball and is unwound gradually as work progresses. It will also be the Filler Cord for all background work and becomes the Working Cord for the design. (See Colour Plate B and Fig. 234.)

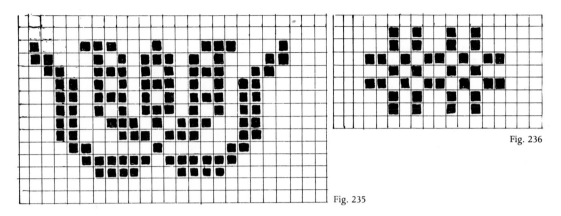

Two pattern ideas for Cavandoli Work

Fig. 235

Fig. 236

A textured look is obtained when knotting Cavandoli Work in one colour only. The contrast is, naturally, much less obvious.

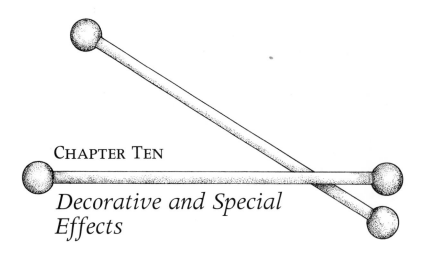

CHAPTER TEN

Decorative and Special Effects

Creating a lace-like effect (Fig. 237)
Small Overhand Knot Picots along the edge of Buttonhole Bars produce a lace-like appearance when worked in fine yarn. The final effect is illustrated in Plate 15 (i) on page 72.

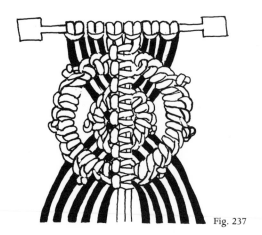

Fig. 237

Unusual three-dimensional technique (Figs. 238–239)
The pictured fringe is based on a piece of work shown in class by one of my students. Apparently made by a man years ago it incorporated a technique which I had never seen before. The unusual raised effect is very striking.

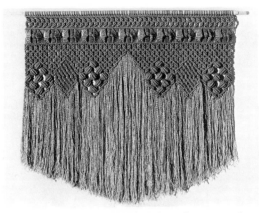

16a *Fringe featuring this three-dimensional technique*

16b *Section of fringe*

TO MAKE SAMPLE

Cut six cords about 27 in (70 cm) long. Set these onto a knot bearer using Lark's Head Knots (see page 20). Bring the cord on the outside left horizontally across all other strands and make a row of Horizontal Cording (see page 28) over it with each of the eleven strands in turn, starting from the left. Divide the twelve cords into two groups of six. Working with the group on the left first bring the cord on the outside right round a pin and place it in a fairly steep diagonal line over the remaining five strands on the left. Make a row of Diagonal Cording (see page 29) over it, using each cord in turn and starting from the right. Place the next strand on the right round a pin and over the remaining four cords on the left. Work a row of Diagonal Cording over it with each strand in turn, starting from the right. With the next cord on the right as Filler Cord make a row of Diagonal Cording with each of the next three strands in turn, starting from the right. Bring the next cord on the right round a pin and over the next two strands on the left. Work two Double Half Hitch Knots over it, starting from the right. Make one more Double Half Hitch Knot, using the next strand on the right as Filler Cord.

The five Filler Cords now become Working Cords and the last used Working Cord on the right now becomes the first Filler Cord. Bring it round a pin on the outside right and place it across the five strands on the left. Using each cord in turn work a row of Horizontal Cording over it, starting from the right. Bring the next cord on the right round a pin and place it over the four strands on the left. Work another row of Horizontal Cording over it with each cord in turn, starting from the right. Using the next cord from the right as Filler Cord make a row of three Double Half Hitch Knots over it, starting from the right, then a row of two over the next cord from the right and finally one over the last cord. Work the second group of strands in the opposite way, then end with a row of Horizontal Cording over all strands, using the cord on the outside right as Filler Cord.

Variations can be produced by combining this technique with additional cords between the two three-dimensional sections. The extra strands could be used to form a Bead Knot (see page 78, Fig. 239 and Plate 16b above).

Reversed Cording (Fig. 240)

This is in fact normal Cording done on the reverse side of work. Knotting occurs in the usual

77

way except that for certain sections the work is turned over and the Cording done on the reverse side. The combination of knotting worked on one side and then the other creates a very interesting textured effect. Solid diamonds of Reversed Cording within ordinary knotting or lines corded on the reverse side are attractive possibilities (see also Fig. 253 on page 84).

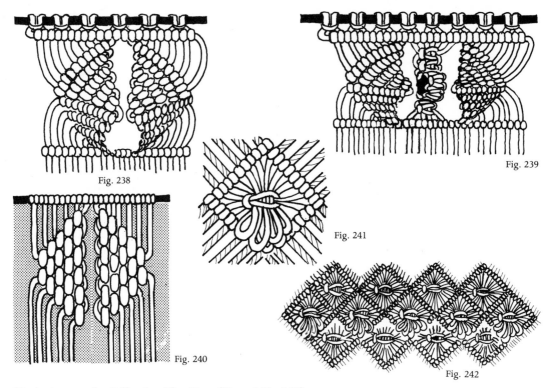

Fig. 238

Fig. 239

Fig. 241

Fig. 240

Fig. 242

Variation on the Collective Flat Knot (Figs. 241–242)
This fancy version of the Collective Flat Knot is very striking and looks particularly elaborate on decorative cushions or evening bags, etc. It often adorns the centre of a diamond shape or a circle. The two outside cords are Working Cords and all centre strands are Filler Cords which are first collectively looped and then a Flat Knot tied over them. The softer materials like wools, dish-cloth cotton or fine cotton yarns, etc. lend themselves best for this purpose.

Just one of these special Collective Knots has been used in the centre of the evening bag pictured on page 79. Beads were threaded onto each single loop before tying the Flat Knot. The ends of the loops were then tightened to a greater or lesser degree to form the attractive beaded group.

Plaited Knot (Fig. 243)
This 'Knot' provides a further variation in the field of textured looks. The technique is more one of interweaving each cord with the previous one rather than knotting as such. A needle is required for the plaiting.

17 Evening bag with matching collar in silver novelty yarn

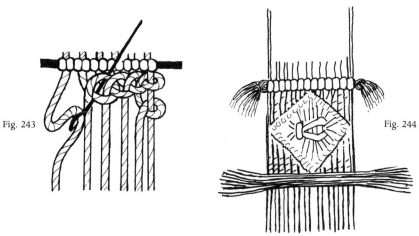

Fig. 243

Fig. 244

Side tassels (Fig. 244)

A tasselled look is given to the side edges of wall hangings with corded dividing lines between pattern sections if these are worked over a number of additional Filler Cords placed across the work. The number of Filler Cords depends on the thickness required for the corded lines and they must, of course, be long enough to be tied with Overhand Knots on either side, leaving sufficient yarn to form tassels. Beads could be threaded over the tassel-ends for decorative purposes, if wished.

18 Wall hanging in wood fibre with side tassels

80

Technique based on Flat Knots (Figs. 245–248)
The following technique is among my personal favourites. It is based on the Flat Knot and looks equally striking in fine and in coarse work. While the basic circular design is occasionally shown in books I have never seen the adaptations illustrated overleaf. Most elaborate patterns in a style of their own emerge when the basic technique is combined with Diagonal Cording (Figs. 251–253).

BASIC TECHNIQUE
To make a basic sample fold six cords in half and mount onto a holding cord or small stick to give twelve working ends (two Filler Cords and ten Working Cords). The two centre cords of the twelve are the Filler Cords. Use one cord from either side of the Filler Cords and tie one Flat Knot over these (Figs. 245–248). Put the two ends of the Working Cords up and out of the way. With the next cord from either side tie a second Flat Knot over the Filler Cords, just below the previous one. Again put the two ends of the Working Cords up and out of the way.

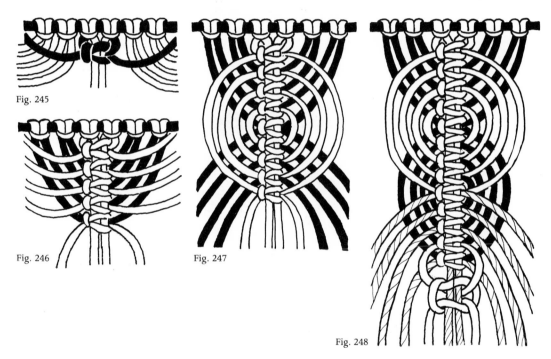

Fig. 245

Fig. 246

Fig. 247

Fig. 248

Repeat with the third cords from either side and then with the fourth cords. Make one more Flat Knot with the remaining two cords but leaving the ends of the Working Cords in a downward position. Now bring down the two Working Cords from the previous Flat Knot (fourth from top) and tie one Flat Knot just below the last one, leaving small half circles at the sides before tightening. Bring down the Working Cords from the third Flat Knot from the top, use these to tie one Flat Knot just below the last one, leaving slightly larger half circles on either side before tightening. Bring down the two Working Cords from the second Flat Knot at the top, tie another Flat Knot just below the last one, leaving still larger half circles at the

81

sides. Repeat with the Working Cords from the top Flat Knot. This completes the pattern and there should now be four graduating circles. More cords are used to make a larger pattern, but the longer the threads of the half circles the less likely it is that they will stay in place and keep their shape.

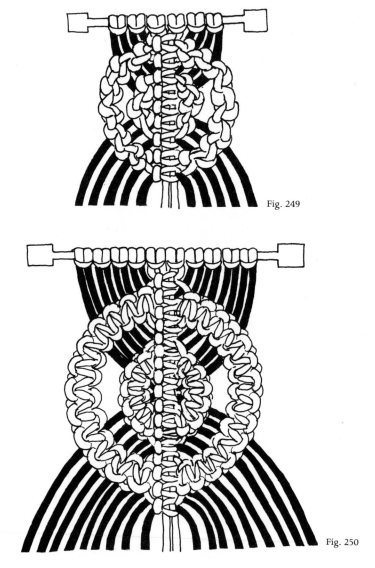

Fig. 249

Fig. 250

Two very effective adaptations and methods for producing larger 'circles' successfully are shown in Figs. 249 and 250. The first half of the pattern is knotted in the usual way or over a larger number of cords, and Sinnets are worked on the side cords before forming the half circles and taking the Working Cords down to make Flat Knots over the Filler Cords.

19 Wall hanging with natural cones incorporating a technique based on Flat Knots

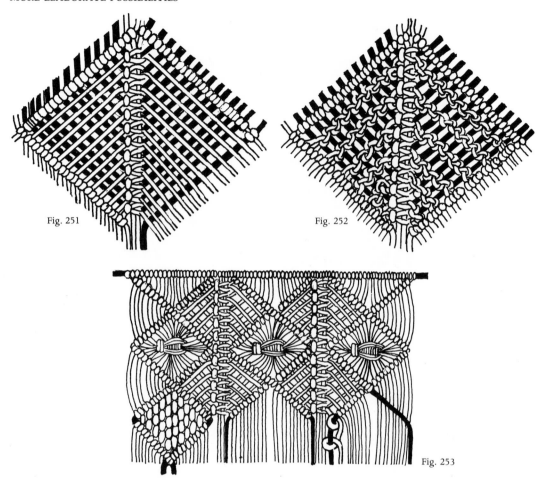

Fig. 251

Fig. 252

Fig. 253

Suggested centres for diamond shapes
The sampler illustrated on page 85 is designed to provide ideas for 'filling in' the centres of diamond shapes. The great variety of possibilities is not always obvious to the beginner.

Oval corded pattern with Collective Flat Knot centre (Figs 254–258)
This pattern can be worked with eight, ten or more cords. When using eight cords, leave one strand on the outside left and right unworked (Figs. 254–258). Place the next cord from either side over and against each other to form a double Filler Cord. Hold firmly to the right and in turn make one Double Half Hitch Knot (see page 28) over the double Filler Cord, using the four strands in the centre as Working Cords and starting from the left. To tighten pull the ends of the Filler Cords out to the left and right respectively. With the two unworked strands in turn make one more Double Half Hitch Knot over the left- and right-hand Filler Cords respectively, aiming at a slightly rounded shape. With the four cords in the centre tie one Flat Knot (see

page 23). Bring the Filler Cord on the outside left round to the right and make one Double Half Hitch Knot over it with the next strand on the right. Work the right-hand side to match. Leave the cord on the outside left and right unworked, place the next strand from either side over and against each other and again use the four centre cords in turn to make Double Half Hitch Knots over the double Filler Cord, starting from the left. To complete and tighten the pattern pull the ends of the Filler Cords out to the left and right respectively.

This pattern can be alternated to create a fabric or one worked below another to form a kind of braid.

20a A variety of knotted centres for diamond shapes   *20b Detail from 20a*

When using ten or twelve cords to give a larger oval, two strands may initially be left unworked at the sides. These will then in turn make one Double Half Hitch Knot over the Filler Cords at the sides. Six or eight strands may be used to make a Collective Flat Knot in the centre before the second half of the pattern is worked.

A corded line interrupted at regular intervals is obtained by using the two outside strands of a group of four or more cords as Filler Cords, placing these over and against each other, as above, and working Double Half Hitch Knots over the double Filler Cords with the two or more centre strands. To tighten pull the ends of the Filler Cords out to the left and right respectively.

It is possible to alternate these corded lines to form a pattern (see second section from the bottom on Plate 3, page 27).

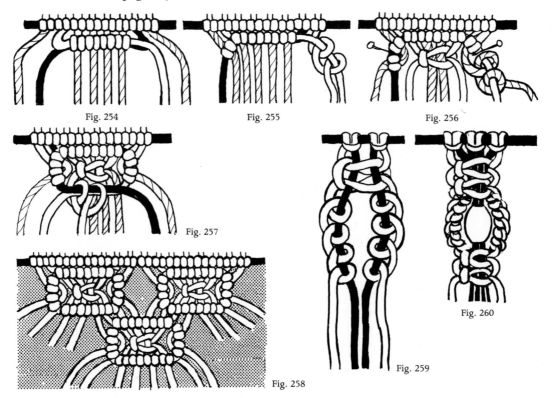

Fig. 254

Fig. 255

Fig. 256

Fig. 257

Fig. 260

Fig. 259

Fig. 258

Rosebuds (Figs. 259–260)

A pattern sometimes called Rosebuds is occasionally seen on plant pot hangers or wall hangings. The basic form is worked over four cords. Start with one Flat Knot, then use the strand on the outside left to make seven or eight Half Hitch Knots over one Filler Cord. With the strand on the outside right work seven or eight Half Hitch Knots over the second Filler Cord and join the two Half Hitch sections (Buttonhole Bars) with one Flat Knot (Fig. 259).

As an alternative the Half Hitch Knots could be worked over a larger number of Filler Cords and/or two strands be brought down the centre to take an oval bead before ending with a Flat Knot (Fig. 260).

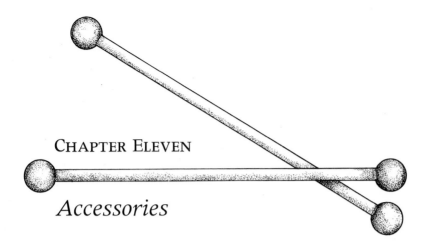

CHAPTER ELEVEN

Accessories

The enjoyment of Macramé goes far beyond tying knots in yarns and creating patterns. Collecting accessories, either useful or decorative, can be a fascinating pastime, especially on a day out, on holiday or a trip abroad.

On the beach you will find all sorts of pebbles, some with holes, providing a ready-made anchorage for your cords to hold them in place. Pebbles can be an unusual and interesting addition to abstract work. They must, of course, not be too large and heavy. The mountains are a source for odd-shaped pieces of wood, attractive small stones and various kinds of pine or fircones. The beds of mountain streams hold such treasures as beautifully shaped pieces of roots and branches which have been swept away. Lakes provide lovely driftwood. In foreign lands there are often unusual everlasting seeds from trees and plants to be found. Rainy days may be spent going round shops looking for beads, wooden items or any other suitable material, not forgetting—of course—the yarns themselves.

Beads
Beads are perhaps the most frequently used accessory in Macramé work. Large chunky beads are particularly suitable for pieces made up in jute or sisal and any other thick yarn. Smaller beads are introduced in fine work and the shiny glass type are best for elaborate jewellery and evening bags. Whatever the purpose make certain that the holes of beads are large enough to take cords. Wooden beads can be opened out either with a drill or the pointed blade of a pair of old scissors. Beads can be introduced in a set pattern at regular intervals or at random. They look very effective when placed where work comes together to a central point. Heavily beaded endings to wall hangings look luscious (see Plate 15k).

21 A selection of useful and ornamental accessories for Macramé

MAKING YOUR OWN BEADS

Stationers and crafts shops nowadays sell a clay-like material which can be formed into beads of varying sizes and shapes. Large enough holes are one of the advantages of making your own beads. Pierce these with a large knitting needle or pointed stick. Place several beads on one knitting needle and rest the ends on two pieces of wood positioned at the right distance. This prevents the beads from sticking to any surface. Several knitting needles will be required if a fairly large number of beads are to be made. Various textures can be given to these by using instruments like an old comb to make lines or dots, etc. When dry paint the beads with poster paint and later coat with matt or glossy varnish. Leave for several days for the varnish to harden completely. Your local potter may be willing to make up ceramic beads for you should you prefer this.

With the ever-increasing interest in Macramé work a much larger selection of suitable beads is gradually becoming available from shops.

THREADING ON BEADS

This is made easier by dipping cord-ends into fabric glue and letting these dry to stiffen. A twisting action instead of trying to push the strands straight through the holes often helps. Cords can sometimes be pulled through with a crochet hook. If no satisfactory solution can be found there only remains tying the beads in the required position with a thread or very fine wire.

Decorative accessories

DECORATIVE RINGS

Rings of all descriptions, provided they are attractive, can be introduced as a decoration. Wooden curtain rings now back in fashion are available in many colours as well as natural light and dark wood. Rings of this kind are very pleasing and need not be covered. Simply fasten them at top and bottom or top only with a Double Half Hitch Knot. Some bangles from jewellery counters are fairly reasonably priced and may just be what you are looking for.

OTHER DECORATIVE ACCESSORIES

brass and copper bells (for hangings
and bellpulls)
interesting knot bearers like:
  old keys
  toasting forks
  chains
  cooking spoons
  pieces of wrought iron
  curtain or carpet rods
bag handles
belt buckles and clasps
frames for firescreens, magazine
racks, plant troughs and screens, etc.
small sized mirrors

22 *Jute wall hanging illustrating
use of decorative accessories*

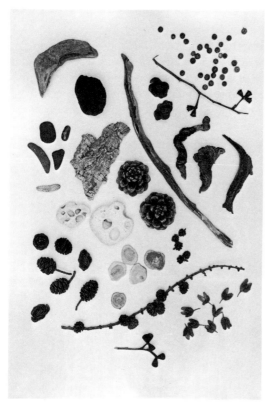

23 A variety of natural materials to collect

24 Beaded wall hanging in fine jute with 'stag horns' as focal point

Natural materials

These are to my mind the most fascinating pieces to collect because they are individual and very personal. They often have a history and remind one perhaps of a holiday or a place you have visited. What to collect:

interesting pieces of wood, driftwood for knot bearers or focal points

branches of dry gorse or heather and other unusual branches

pieces of roots

bamboo canes (these may also be cut into pieces and used as a form of bead)

large and small cones (fir, pine, cryptomeria, etc.)

everlasting seeds from unusual trees or plants

cork

bottle corks

small stones and pebbles

nuts and nut shells

dried flowers, grasses and seedheads

90

Useful accessories

basket cane to work over or for making rings and ovals

rings for working over, curtain rings for fine work, large metal or wooden rings as a base for focal points or anchorage in vertical work like plant hangers (see 'How to insert a ring' on page 66)

dowelling, split cane, kebab sticks and skewers for supports (make certain that these are straight)

pipe cleaners and flower wire for support or strengthening of edges

containers like plant pots, waste paper baskets and tins to be covered with yarn

plastic piping to be cut into sections for serviette rings

rubber bands and washing pegs for holding work in place when covering shaped containers

razor blades for splicing basket cane

needles with large eyes for sewing ends into the back of work or to put cords through confined spaces

fabric glue for concealing cord-ends at the back of work and joining cords, etc.

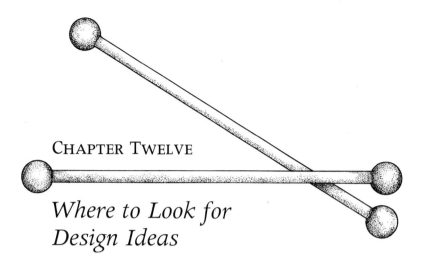

CHAPTER TWELVE

Where to Look for Design Ideas

A distinction between a good and a bad design can surely apply to practical and functional pieces of work only. Ornamental items are largely a matter of taste and have to appeal to the individual. For this reason, a variety of projects is shown in this section, ranging from traditional to abstract pieces.

MAKING UP YOUR OWN DESIGN

Many people are not aware of the full potential of Macramé design or remain content with copying work from books, because they are not confident enough to be creative in their own right. To have designed a piece of work oneself is a very satisfying experience, particularly for people who were convinced that they possessed no artistic flair of their own. Macramé, almost without fail, brings hidden talents to the fore and provided you have studied the theories of the craft well, there is no reason why you should not soon produce a masterpiece of your own. One of the great rewards in teaching Macramé is students' sudden discovery of a creative ability they never dreamt they had. A number of guidelines are given below to assist you when setting out to make a decorative piece of work, like a wall hanging.

1. Study first the place where it will hang
2. Determine the size
3. Choose suitable material in keeping with the surroundings (jute and sisal do not particularly complement an antique or traditional décor, nor is lace-like work the best choice for an ultra-modern home)
4. When using more than one colour remember that multiple colours distract from the intricacy of the actual knotting pattern. If you primarily want to show off your knotted work use natural or one colour yarn only

5. Look for an interesting knot bearer (see 'Accessories' on page 89) complementary to the yarn and the surroundings
6. Before cutting cords determine the kind of design and pattern. A closely worked piece takes more yarn than a more open one (see 'Length of cords' on page 19)
7. Allow extra yarn for the Working Cords of long Sinnet patterns and also for cords to be taken across the work as Filler Cords for dividing lines or at any point where it is obvious that especially long Working Cords are required

The interest in Macramé is not solely confined to knotting—it also captures one's imagination when looking for design ideas.

Samplers

A sampler of basic knots and knot combinations is described in the section for guided pieces of work in this book (see page 126) as a kind of learning piece which will turn into an attractive wall hanging. Samplers of this kind are always appealing, very varied to do and can be adapted to any size of square or rectangle. Extra interest is added by introducing beads or by working Sinnet patterns alternately with more fabric-like sections. Long slim samplers can hang and look good in narrow spaces such as between two doors or at the side of a piece of furniture (see Plate 25).

25 Long sampler for confined space

93

Building up a design

Many of my wall hangings have been 'built up' inasmuch as I have simply put a certain number of cords onto a knot bearer, sometimes two or three colours, embarking on a random design. Working knots and patterns in various directions, incorporating perhaps beads and/or interesting natural materials, can soon result in fascinating textures. It is impossible to give working instructions for 'built-up' projects of this type but the hanging shown in Colour Plate G is intended as an example.

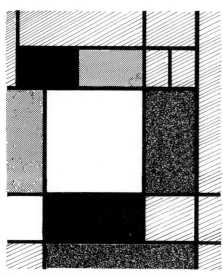

Fig. 261

26 *Jute wall hanging based on a painting by Piet Mondrian*

Design ideas from the arts (Figs. 261–264)

Books and magazines of this kind are excellent for design inspiration. Horizontal, vertical and diagonal lines lend themselves best for Macramé work and these are, therefore, what to look for. Circles and ovals are relatively easy to achieve by working over a solid base like wooden or metal rings, curtain rings, circles made of basket cane, etc. Fig 261 represents a painting by the Dutch painter Piet Mondrian. Many of his 'Compositions' could be translated into unusual Macramé samplers. A different pattern may be used in each rectangle and Sinnets to mark the dividing lines. In the knotted example shown in Plate 26 each square or rectangle in Mondrian's painting is represented. Slight adaptations are necessary, as a rule, to allow for certain patterns requiring particular numbers of cords.

During a lecture on 'Art Nouveau', the style of the eighteen-nineties with its patterns of curving lines, I felt the sudden desire to try and do with string what the artists of that time had done with paint or metal. An example of the Art Nouveau style is illustrated by Fig 262. The curved lines on the left-hand striped hanging in Colour Plate C are worked over basket cane. The project was done on a large board placed against a wall. Three or four loops were pinned in position at a time and the cords knotted over. It soon became obvious that an abstract pattern had to be worked between the cane loops as on the inside of these the cords came together dramatically while on the outside they opened out in a fan-like fashion. Art Nouveau having been followed by abstract art makes this an interesting combination.

Fig. 262

Fig. 263

The German artist Paul Klee has painted a number of pictures of almost string-like rows of houses. These have a child-like kind of appeal and I have tried to capture this in the Macramé collage pictured in Plate 27. A number of my students have knotted houses since and have produced astonishingly successful pieces of string architecture. The buildings could be given a doll's-house type of appearance by putting small coloured felt curtains behind the windows and ornamenting the church with simulated 'stained glass', etc.

27 Macramé collage inspired by drawings of string-like houses by Paul Klee

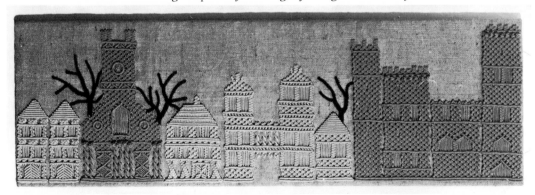

The idea for the larger right-hand wall hanging pictured in Colour Plate C also came from a painting by Paul Klee. The simple outlines of a fish are easily reproduced with Cording and to give the scene a tropical touch bits of coloured jute have been introduced in the tails and fins.

Fig. 264

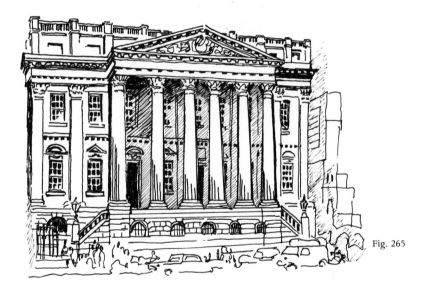

Fig. 265

Inspiration from architecture (Fig. 265)
The outlines of many buildings could serve as a basic pattern for Macramé work. Some of their features, too, like the arrangement of the beams on Tudor-style houses, provide us with the basic shapes we are looking for.

The façade of the Mansion House in London inspired the hanging in Plate 28. It is executed in nylon fishing twine. The relative proportions have been narrowed down in order to make it more elegant.

96

A Chinese-type lantern in fine cotton twine and wrought-iron flower trough covered with a pattern in two colours

B Tiffany lampshade with matching jar covered in turquoise dish-cloth cotton. Three examples of Cavandoli work

C Wall hangings in jute with
curved lines based on the Art
Nouveau style, and with fish
design inspired by a painting of
Paul Klee's

D Oval design with beads and
Macramé-edged mirror. Handbag
with matching belt in cotton
twine

E Wrought-iron firescreen covered in a three-colour pattern. Sculptured head in natural cotton twine

F A selection of knotted belts

G Abstract hanging in three colours worked in jute and natural materials. Large plant pot hanger in thick jute

H Wall hanging in bleached and brown jute and matching lampshade in brown, beige and while wool

28 Knotted wall panel in nylon fishing twine based on architectural design

Ideas from interior design (Figs. 266–267)

The elaborate ceilings and wall panels of stately homes and historic buildings never fail to attract my attention. The design for the wall hanging shown in Plate 29 is taken from the drawing-room ceiling of a stately home in Sussex which was featured in a magazine. After sketching the basic shape I made up the Macramé version. Some of the proportions were altered to allow for certain patterns requiring particular numbers of cords. Fig. 267 shows another ceiling design.

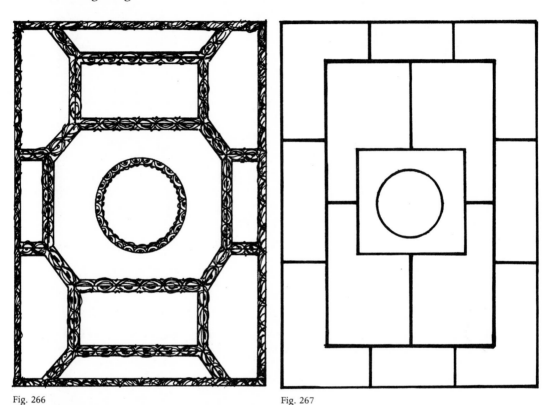

Fig. 266   Fig. 267

Looking at antique furniture (Figs. 268–269)

Furniture design can provide many interesting outlines suitable for knotted projects, in particular antique and traditional pieces. The leaded glass patterns in cabinets as shown on page 101 usually consist of horizontal, vertical and diagonal lines and are, therefore, very suitable. Fig. 268 and Fig. 269 show two pattern ideas taken from lead work in glass. Old-fashioned writing desks, chests of drawers and chairbacks should be looked at too.

Three-dimensional hangings.

These may be a combination of artistic ability and knotting skill or merely a piece of imaginative fun like the hanging illustrated on page 100. It is made up from nylon yarn comparable in thickness to rug wool but softer, blended with four colours of raffia. The mounting is done on an odd-shaped piece of wood and the trimmings are children's beads.

29 Wall hanging in nylon fishing twine with the shape of a stately home ceiling

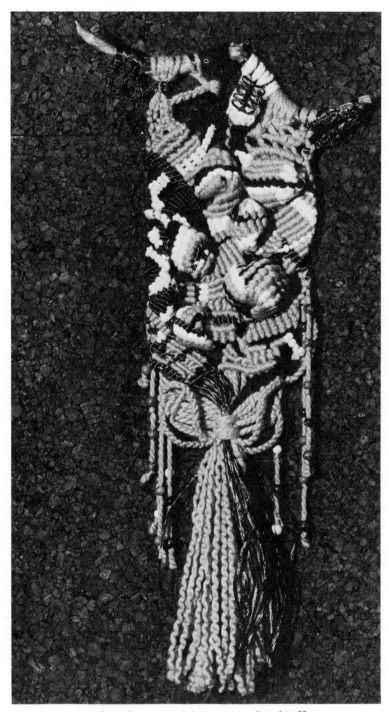

30 Three-dimensional design in wool and raffia

Three-dimensional effects are normally obtained by incorporating pieces of wood, thick rings or shapes made from basket cane, etc. No solid bases have been used for the hanging in Plate 30. At certain points corded sections are worked over a number of strands, sometimes to the left or to the right, long enough to be folded up and over or to the side to form a kind of twisted loop. The Working Cords are taken down on the reverse side and are brought back into the work at a suitable point. The areas in between the three-dimensional sections are knotted in a random design.

Fig. 268

Fig. 269

Pictorial hangings

To make a pictorial piece of Macramé is one of the more difficult aspects of the craft and is normally only achieved by working Double Half Hitch Knots in various directions. The finish is much more tapestry-like than the usual knotted work and is similar in a way to Cavandoli Work (see page 74). A partly pictorial effect is obtained in the wall hanging pictured on page 103 (left). The background consists of leaves, branches and fruit, depicting a tree with two owls sitting in it.

Design by chance

Once you have become an ardent knotter, friends with bright ideas may well make a few suggestions as to what you could be doing next. 'Why don't you make an Oval?' I was asked one day. The end of a beautiful friendship was a real possibility on several occasions while I set about this challenge. The very shape of an oval brings all the cords to the centre and there comes a point when work has to be superimposed and strands sewn in the back. As a result I learned that superimposed work is not only a possibility but that it is at the same time very attractive. (See Colour Plate D.)

Knotting a daydream
The odd-shaped pieces of fired clay incorporated in the right-hand hanging on page 103 were given to me by a pottery teacher. I decided to treat these as rocks. The rugged scenery of the mountains is re-created by areas of Small Shell Knots through which the stream, originating from various sources, winds its way over the 'rocks' before ending in a cascade.

Fig. 270

Macramé sculpture (Fig. 270)
Macramé sculpture is a challenge and fun to do. Pieces are best worked over a solid base. A wig stand serves as a base in the case of the sculptured head in Colour Plate E. The basic idea is taken from a history book and dates back to Assyrian times. It was considered particularly appropriate since the knot in its decorative form on clothing originated during that period. The sculpture represents the head of an Assyrian worshipper and is worked from the point with the back of the helmet knotted in separately. The base of the helmet is executed in the round. The hair and beard are worked in Bead Knots and Small Shell Knots respectively. The cord-ends are neatly glued to the base of the stand and covered with a piece of felt. (See colour Plate E.)

102

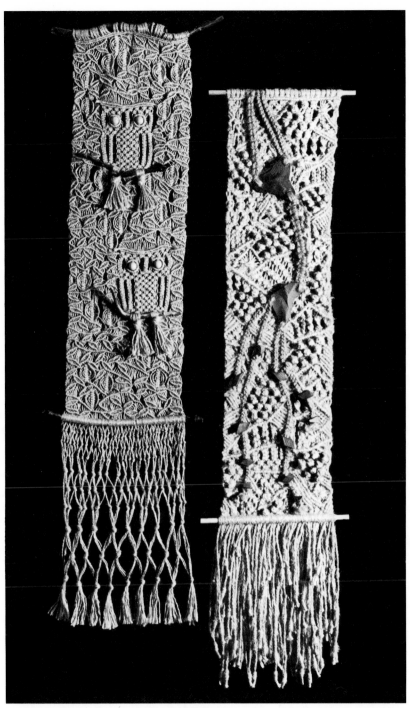

31 Pictorial design with owls (left) and 'Knotted Daydream' (right), both worked in jute

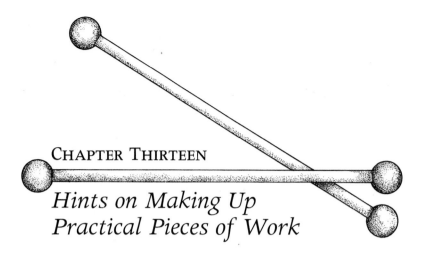

CHAPTER THIRTEEN

*Hints on Making Up
Practical Pieces of Work*

Belts
(see Colour Plate F)
Belts made up in long unattached Sinnets or sections of loose unworked cords are unsatisfactory when in use due to folding over or overlapping of work. This should be considered when copying designs from books. For best results choose either fairly firm patterns or work solid sections at intervals in order to avoid disappointment. Firm edges too contribute to the neat look of a belt.

TIE BELTS
Longer or shorter cord-ends are needed for fastening belts of this nature as no clasps or buckles are involved. Allow for this when cutting cords. When the knotted belt is placed round the waist sufficient space must be left between the beginning and the end to accommodate the knot for fastening. Cord-ends may be trimmed with beads or with Coil Knots (see page 43). If the strands are to be set onto a holding cord proceed as for 'Starting with a fringe' (see page 122) and take the two ends of the holding cord straight into the pattern at the sides.

BELTS WITH BUCKLES (Figs. 271–279)
The cross bar of the buckle serves as knot bearer. The required length cords are normally set on with Lark's Head Knots in preference to Double Half Hitch Knots. The reason for this is that more strands can be accommodated, often making the belt look in better proportion to the size of the buckle. Setting on with Double Half Hitch Knots (Picot fashion, see page 47) may require additional strands to be joined in (see page 105). It is, however, necessary to make certain that the belt will not be too wide to be threaded through the buckle comfortably.

Belts worked in the Alternate Flat Knot Pattern or similar present no problems when matching the overlap with the knotting beneath once the end has been taken through the buckle. This is not so when working diamond shapes or other individual rather than continuous patterns. In order to position a complete diamond shape or other design in the centre of the buckle (which will hide the cross bar and the Lark's Head Knot beginning), with the overlap matching the work beneath, the first section immediately after the mounting must consist of half a diamond shape or other half pattern only. This half pattern should be as shallow as possible to allow for the space taken up by the cross bar (Fig. 274). If a belt is to be made up alternately of some more open and more closed sections, it is essential to begin with half a solid pattern. This again ensures the successful covering of the mounting bar when the belt is threaded through and a matching overlap.

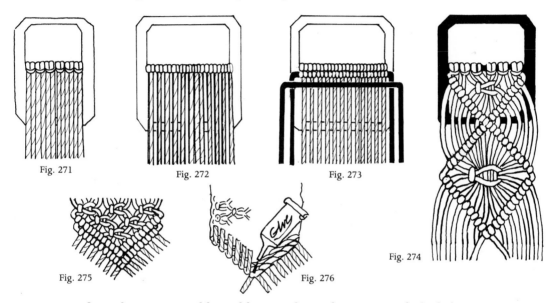

Fig. 271

Fig. 272

Fig. 273

Fig. 275

Fig. 276

Fig. 274

One way of avoiding any possible problems with overlaps is to work the belt in the chosen pattern, changing over to the Alternate Flat Knot Pattern about 3 to 4 in (8 to 10 cm) before the point where the belt is threaded through the buckle and finishing in this way. The contrast between the patterned sides and back and the plain piece taken through the buckle and forming the overlap is very striking.

Belt-ends are to advantage finished to a point with an edging of two or three rows of Cording. This gives a firm finish to which cord-ends can be glued at the back. Apply fabric glue on the reverse side of this corded edge, then neatly align all cord-ends and pin until dry. Press down firmly as the glue starts to harden.

To hold the belt overlap in place work a Sinnet of Flat Knots or other Sinnet, long enough to form a loop right round the double thickness of the belt. Turn the loop inside out and join by sewing the ends in the back. Turn the loop back onto the right side and slide it over the belt end. Position where required (Figs. 277–279).

A straight corded edge could be worked as an alternative ending with the cord-ends glued to the back or leaving a small fringe.

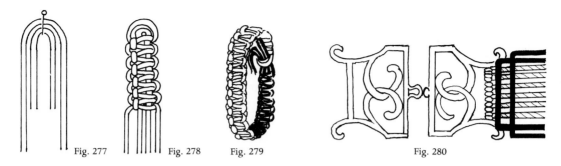

Fig. 277   Fig. 278   Fig. 279   Fig. 280

BELTS MOUNTED ON CLASPS (Fig. 280)

Belts mounted on clasps have no overlap and both the beginning and the ending are visible. These, therefore, have to match. Setting on with Lark's Head Knots is unsuitable in this instance as there is no satisfactory way to attach the cord-ends to the second half of the clasp in a similar fashion. Mounting with Double Half Hitch Knots (see 'Picots' on page 47) is preferable. This presents no problems the other end as the cords can easily be attached with a row of Cording worked over the bar of the clasp to match the beginning. However, this kind of mounting does not always give sufficient strands for a belt of the desired width in relation to the size of the clasp. To counteract this new cords have to be added immediately after setting on (Fig. 280).

Decrease the number of strands at the other end by leaving out cords at the sides as shown under 'Working to a point' on page 55, thereby making the two ends correspond. The left out cords at the sides are eventually sewn into the back of work and the remaining strands attached to the second half of the clasp with Double Half Hitch Knots. Knot off two strands at a time with Overhand Knots making certain that these are well concealed at the back. Dab a little fabric glue onto each knot to make these more secure and trim all ends.

Handbags and evening bags

These can be worked in a multitude of different yarns, designs and patterns. Jute and sisal are ideal for larger shoppers or holiday tote bags, cotton twines for smart every-day bags and tubular rayon, silver, gold and coloured novelty yarns for most attractive evening purses. Choose suitable material, bearing in mind the function of the bag. If unlined or with a thin lining only, a fairly solid pattern should be worked, the yarn having to carry the weight of the contents. Leather-based bags or holdalls with heavy linings may be made up in finer yarns and fairly open, ornamental patterns. In this instance, the knotting is purely decorative and the weight of any shopping is carried by the lining. It is essential to keep the worked areas as straight as possible, in particular the side edges, and it is recommended that the lines on the knotting board are constantly observed as a guide to check that all patterns are in their correct horizontal and vertical place. Twisting can occur if attention is not paid to this. For sections which need knotting or sewing together see 'Joining sections together' on page 64 and 'Edges' on page 65.

The design possibilities for Macramé bags are almost unlimited and ideas may be taken from leather, plastic and material bags in shops. Many can be successfully adapted to string work.

The following comments and drawings are intended to help you with your projects:

106

32 A selection of knotted bags

KNOTTED HANDLES TAKEN STRAIGHT INTO WORK (Figs. 281–282)

This is a very neat and secure way of attaching handles and eliminates the sometimes tedious and difficult task of sewing these on. It is essential to calculate cords long enough for making the handles, allowing at the same time extra yarn to be taken into the work for the bag itself (see 'Length of cords' on page 19). If the handles are of a Sinnet type, each single Working Cord must be at least five times the length of the Filler Cords and possibly up to seven times if the handles have to be very strong and the Working Cords are required to cover a large number of Filler Cords.

TO KNOT HANDLES

Once the cord lengths have been established and the strands cut, leave sufficient yarn unworked at one end to be taken into the bag pattern, then knot the handle to the required length. The cord-ends left unworked at the beginning and those remaining at the end are eventually knotted onto the holding cord(s) used for the bag and taken straight into the pattern. To make a double holding cord see Figs. 283 and 284.

When calculating cord numbers for the bag itself allow for the strands from the handles coming into the work. Similarly, if the ends from the holding cord(s) eventually become(s) part of the pattern. If the bag is worked in the round the knotting board becomes obsolete. Cut a double thickness of corrugated cardboard to the required shape and size, giving a base to work over. A small cushion or a towel could be pushed between the two layers if more bulk is necessary. Boxes from your local grocers will provide the cardboard.

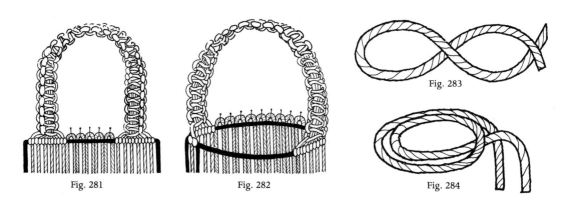

Fig. 281
Fig. 282
Fig. 283
Fig. 284

BAGS WITH HANDLE TO FORM SIDE PIECES AND BASE (Figs. 285–288)

For bags worked in two halves cut two holding cords for each side to the same length as the Working Cords for the bag itself, adding extra yarn for the holding cords to be taken across the width of the work at the top (about 12–20 in (30–50 cm)). When the Working Cords are mounted bring the ends of the holding cords straight into the pattern at the sides. This needs taking into account when calculating numbers of strands. Once the front and the back sections are completed knot the handle long enough to be taken round the sides and along the lower edge. Join the two ends of the strap neatly and position the seam along the base of the bag. Sew or knot all pieces together (see 'Joining sections together' on page 64).

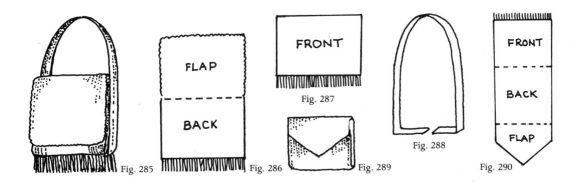

Fig. 285 Fig. 286 Fig. 287 Fig. 288 Fig. 289 Fig. 290

FINISHING HOLDALLS OR BAGS WITH A BASE

This method is described under 'things to make' on page 170. When the holdall has reached the required length (either knotted in the round or in two halves sewn together) work about two rows of Horizontal Cording right round the lower edge before starting to knot the actual base itself.

Note: The number of cords left unworked at the sides varies according to the thickness of the yarn used. Thinner yarns require a greater number of unworked strands. Whatever the number the corded rows should always be two less, i.e. if twelve strands are left out, ten rows of Horizontal Cording are required (five on the front and five at the back). The difference is made up by the knotting together of the two sections. The extra Filler Cords for the Cording on each half must be five times that of the width of the holdall.

ENVELOPE BAGS OR PURSES (Figs. 289–295)

These are relatively easy to do as they are generally made up in one single piece. Knotting may start from either end. If you start with the flap cord-ends are sewn or glued to the inside of the bag and concealed by the lining (Figs. 289–290).

Working from the other end provides the alternative of finishing either with a fringe along the edge of the flap or glueing the ends to the back. To conceal glued ends work several rows of Cording along the edge of the flap to serve as a foundation for the cords to adhere to. In the latter instance lining is necessary to hide the glue finish (Figs. 291–295).

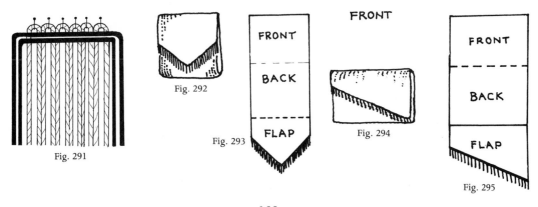

Fig. 291 Fig. 292 Fig. 293 Fig. 294 Fig. 295

BAGS WITH OVAL OR CIRCULAR HANDLES MADE OF WOOD OR PLASTIC (Fig. 296)

The back and front sections of bags of this kind are worked separately to a certain point in order to obtain a manageable size of opening. The two sides are then joined together and work continues in the round over a corrugated cardboard base as described under 'Bags with knotted handles taken straight into work' on page 108. If preferred, the two sections may be knotted separately and then sewn together at the sides. Cords are set straight onto the handles with Lark's Head Knots and generally Sinnets of at least twelve Flat Knots (depending on the thickness of the yarn) or other Sinnets are worked to ensure an adequate opening before the actual bag pattern is commenced. Due to the oval or circular shape of the handles the Sinnets will automatically spread out in a fan-like fashion. If a close texture is required from this point additional cords must be added immediately. Joining the two sides together with a corded line, at the same time adding new strands at intervals, is one of the neatest methods (Fig. 296). If the bag is to become wider still as the pattern progresses new cords will have to be joined in at a later stage.

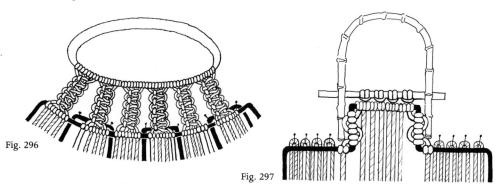

Fig. 296

Fig. 297

STRAIGHT WOODEN OR METAL BAG HANDLES

All cords are mounted along the base of straight handles. This can be done either with Lark's Head Knots or with Double Half Hitch Knots Picot fashion (see page 47). The first method is preferable if a larger number of strands is to be mounted. The second is used when the mounting rod is to be covered completely. To increase the number of cords for the pattern area the same procedure could be followed as for 'Belts mounted on Clasps' (see page 106). The beginning of bags of this kind is again worked in two halves to ensure a sufficiently large opening before the two sides are joined and work continues in the round. Alternatively the two sides can be knotted separately and then sewn together, leaving enough space at the top for the bag to open comfortably.

BAMBOO HANDLES WITH STRAIGHT METAL RODS ALONG THE BASE (Fig. 297)

This kind of handle is readily available in many sizes but presents the problem that the bamboo ends on either side extend below the rod. This limits the number of cords to be mounted. Immediate shaping can therefore not take place. A neat solution is to set on as many strands as possible, then placing the midway point of a separate Filler Cord just below the rod with the two cord-ends out to the sides (this Filler Cord should be about 12–20 in (30–50 cm) longer than the set on strands). A row of Horizontal Cording is then worked over this Filler

110

Cord (Fig. 297) followed by the selected pattern. At either end of the pattern rows a Vertical Double Half Hitch Knot is tied until the knotting is level with the bamboo ends. Bring the ends of the Filler Cord out to the left and right respectively, below the bamboo ends and set on a further number of strands on either side. Make certain that the ultimate overall number of cords is right for the pattern.

ADAPTING BAG DESIGNS TO MACRAMÉ WORK (Figs. 298–305)

Many appealing handbag designs may be re-created in knotting with some possible adaptations. Some can be worked in one piece and others in several individual sections which are eventually sewn or knotted together. The following examples are given to show various possibilities.

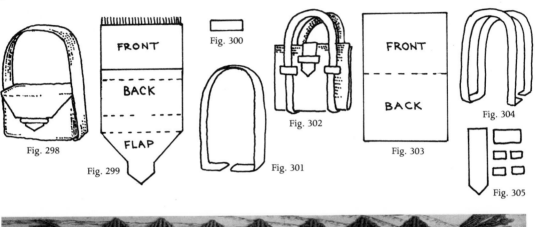

33 *Table mat knotted in dish-cloth cotton*

111

Table mats

Macramé table mats are very beautiful and different. Cotton twine and coloured dish-cloth cotton are particularly suitable materials to use. The more intricate patterns naturally complement dainty, elegant table ware while bolder designs are more in keeping with rougher, earthenware crockery. Place mats are best started and finished with a fringe. It is easy enough to begin in the ordinary way but problems arise the other end when a large number of cords are left which somehow have to disappear. Sometimes we are told to sew these neatly in the back of work. It is very difficult to accommodate a great many strands without stretching and pulling the work out of shape quite apart from the tedious time one would spend trying. Cord-ends could be glued to the reverse side but this may present problems when washing.

STARTING PLACE MATS WITH A FRINGE
(See 'Starting with a fringe' on page 122). The holding cord for table mats may be cut the same length as the Working Cords plus twice the width of the mat. The two ends of the holding cord are taken straight into the work at the sides. The extra length allowed is calculated to go across the width of the mat at the top for setting on the strands and for the Filler Cord taken across all strands at the end of work (Fig. 306).

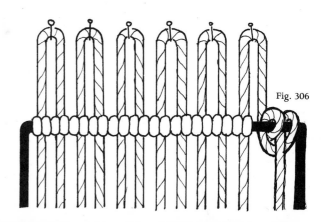

Fig. 306

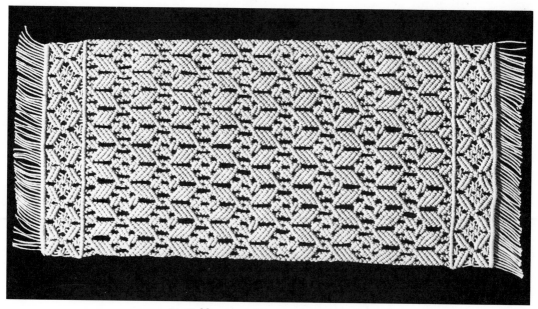

34 Table runner in natural cotton twine

Lampshades (Figs. 307–310)

Knotted lampshades are extremely effective. They can be worked to look like lace for bedrooms and antique décors or given a more rustic appearance for more modern surroundings. Great care must be taken when selecting a base to work over. Lampshade frames are often hopelessly out of true and the distance between any two struts may vary considerably. One section will, therefore, require more cords to cover than the next which immediately creates problems when several identical panels are to be knotted. Only small variations can be overcome without too much difficulty. Straight-sided shades are easiest to make up. For conical or Tiffany-type frames the patterns need gradual opening out unless new cords are added. A Picot mounting greatly enhances the effect of lampshades. Bind all struts if they are not to be incorporated in the knotting. Generally, these are, however, covered with one of the Macramé Sinnets. Each section is then knotted in turn and, if wished, attached to the side Sinnets at regular intervals as work progresses. Tatted Bars or Flat Knot Sinnets are the best choice for this as they provide convenient loops to fasten work to. It is important to start the Sinnets alternately, one from the left and the next one from the right (Fig. 308). This results in two identical sides of the Sinnets facing each other and the loops will be at even levels so that knotting can take place in straight horizontal lines. Failure to reverse the Sinnets will produce a slightly slanting panel which is unsatisfactory.

Panels need not necessarily be joined to the side Sinnets. In this instance one of the spirals could be used for covering the struts. Attaching sections to this type of Sinnet would interrupt the natural flow of their line. Figs. 309 and 310 show two ways of attaching sections of work to the side Sinnets.

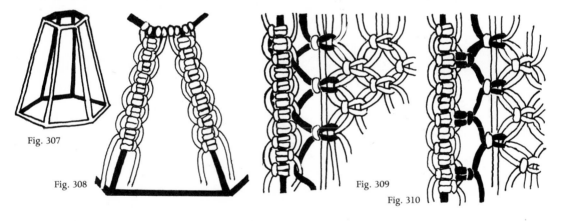

Fig. 307

Fig. 308

Fig. 309

Fig. 310

If a Flat Knot pattern or similar is simply opened out to reach across the widening pattern area the originally set on cords will not be sufficient to cover the wire along the base of the lampshade. Attach the existing strands to the lower edge first and then fill in with extra cords mounted Picot fashion (see page 47), pulling the cord-ends tight to conceal the Picot. Knot off all cords and end with a fringe. A few more rows of pattern could be knotted below the base wire before knotting off. Trim ends with beads if wished and hold in place with Overhand Knots.

Fabric-covered lampshades greatly benefit by the addition of a Macramé fringe along the base and edgings of this kind make a very elegant contribution to the final effect.

Extra cords may be threaded through the loops of the side Sinnets to be taken into the work at the sides. See also page 61, Fig. 200.

LINING LAMPSHADES (Figs. 311–313)
The lining of Macramé lampshades generally distracts from the sometimes very intricate knotting pattern. When unlined, however, the light bulb may be disturbingly obvious. Light diffusers originally seemed to be the answer but these have been described as dangerous and are, therefore, not recommended. For straight-sided shades a thin, unpleated lining is probably the most satisfactory answer. Tinted bulbs sometimes help. The lining for a Tiffany lampshade can be taken straight from the upper wire circle down to the lower edge, thereby leaving some depth between the lining and the knotted work.

The upper wire circle of large ceiling shades is sometimes rather wide and allows for tassels or beaded cords to be attached to on the inside which hang down loosely as a decorative way of disguising the light bulb. The tassels must, however, be at sufficient distance from the bulb to avoid disaster.

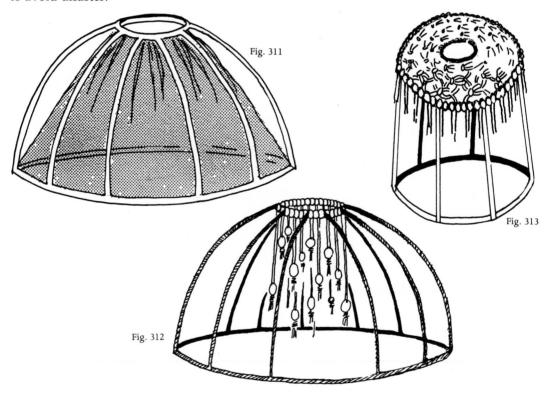

Fig. 311

Fig. 313

Fig. 312

The sometimes rather large openings at the top of lampshades may be reduced by placing a separate, smaller wire circle over the centre. The cords are set onto this and work takes place in a circular fashion. All strands are then attached to the outer wire circle with Double Half Hitch Knots and additional strands set on, if required (Picot fashion), as described earlier.

The lampshade shown in Colour Plate B, has a reduced open area along the base of its frame. A smaller circle is introduced in the centre which will require fewer cords to cover. Tassels are, therefore, left along the outer wire in order to reduce the number of strands. (For illustrations of lampshades see Colour Plates A, B and H.)

Jewellery
The scope for knotted jewellery is tremendous and ranges from very simple chokers and bracelets children can make to most elaborate collar-type necklaces. Some of the recommended silver and gold novelty yarns are uncomfortable when worn against the skin. Gold and silver crochet or knitting yarns are smoother but often have to be worked double to be successful. For coloured jewellery tubular rayon or nylon yarns are most effective. They are rather stretchy to work with and beginners sometimes find difficulty in knotting evenly. Thick crochet yarns could be used instead but may need working double.

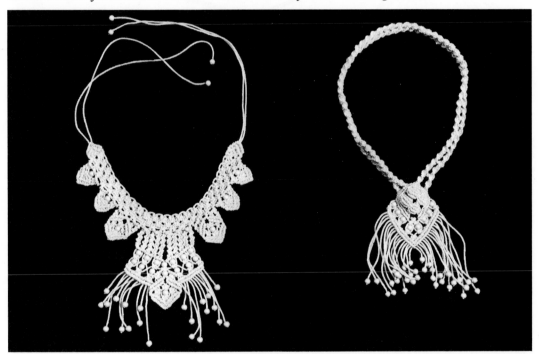

35 Two examples of jewellery in gold novelty yarn

BRACELETS AND CHOKERS
These are in a way miniature belts and are usually knotted as a small version of a tie belt (see 'Tie Belts' on page 104). An alternative to fastening at the back with an ordinary double knot is to make a small Sinnet, formed into a loop, through which the cord-ends are pushed from either side and then tightened. In the case of a choker the ends must be long enough to make it possible for the choker to be slipped over the head. Pushing the cord-ends through a bead in a similar way is a further possibility. Coil Knots or beads may be used to trim the ends and to prevent these from slipping through the looped Sinnet or bead (Fig. 314).

115

COLLAR-TYPE NECKLACES (Figs. 315–316)

The mounting of cords may be done on one or two holding cords, long enough to allow for tying at the back, or on a piece of silvered wire the ends of which can be bent back and hooked over each other to fasten. Ready silvered neckbands are at present available from Department Stores and some smaller shops. Collars of this kind may be knotted in sections at intervals or as an overall pattern by adding new strands as the work opens out. Long tassels should only be left to hang down the centre front. Any tassel-ends at shoulder level will fall forward over the knotted work.

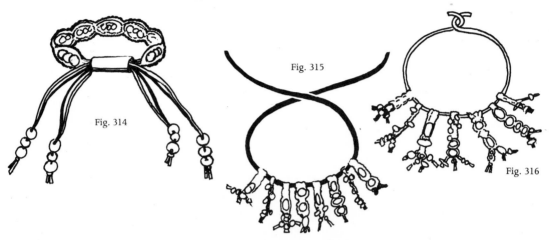

36 Fringe for evening dress in white 3-ply wool

Fringes

Victorian times were the heydays for Macramé fringes. They are still worked today but for different purposes. While they used to adorn fireplaces and four-poster beds they are now found on evening skirts and lampshades. Macramé fringes range from extremely simple to very elaborate designs and can either be knotted separately or straight onto a particular item (see 'Setting on Cords' on page 20). A highly individual touch is given to garments with Macramé trimmings.

The fringe pictured in Plate 36 is designed to be sewn along the base of an evening dress. The material used is white 3-ply wool. The set on cords were 2 yards (1.82 m) long (before folding in half) and the finished fringe measures 10 in (25 cm). The Filler Cords from the Diagonal Cording at the end of each alternate section were knotted into two Single Chains (see page 33), tied together with a kind of bow and held in place with a Flat Knot (see page 22). All cord-ends are knotted off with Overhand Knots, unravelled into separate strands, giving a light and delicate ending.

To ensure correct shaping of fringes for A-line skirts, working over a pattern is recommended. This may be pinned to the knotting board. Cords have to be added in suitable places to allow for the increasing pattern area.

Knotted fringes for lampshades are most effective when worked in tubular rayon. This material does not fray.

Plates 16a and b on page 77 show another example of a fringe.

Firescreens, magazine racks, flower troughs, etc.

Frames for these are usually constructed in wood or wrought iron. The frames shown on Page 118 and in Colour Plates A and E have been made up by blacksmiths to specific designs and sizes. The measurements need to be accurate and variations from one side to another can create problems. Thin rods have been introduced about $\frac{1}{2}$ in ($1\frac{1}{4}$ cm) all along the inside of the basic frame. The cords are attached to these rods on all four sides. The outer frame, therefore, remains unobstructed and serves as a finishing border to offset the knotting. Cords are mounted along the top rod and the work is joined to the sides with Picots (see 'Working Picots over the side edges' on page 65). When the required length is reached attach the cord-ends along the base rod with Double Half Hitch Knots (see page 28). Knot off all strands with Overhand Knots (see page 35) using two to four cords at a time and leave a small fringe (see also Colour Plates A and E).

Covering containers (Figs. 317–319)

Beautiful effects are obtained by covering containers like bottles, jars, waste paper baskets, plant pot holders, tins etc. with Macramé work. Unsightly or damaged containers are best lined on the outside with coloured self-adhesive plastic materials in order to have a clean base to knot over. Plain colours will show off the knotting to best advantage. Work may start at the top with the holding cord or cords taken straight into the knotting pattern. The holding cord must, therefore, be the same length as the Working Cords plus the measurement of the circumference of the container. Hold work in place along the top edge with clothes pegs. Putting a layer of thin foam rubber round the container to which the knotting may be pinned sometimes helps. When the required length is reached end with a row of Cording along the lower edge, remove foam rubber, if used, and neatly glue the cord-ends to the base of the container. Trim and stick a piece of felt or similar over all ends to conceal.

37 *Magazine rack covered with a Macramé pattern in two colours*

38 String-covered containers

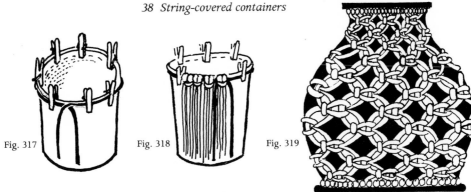

Fig. 317   Fig. 318   Fig. 319

If necessary, carefully glue the knotted work along the top edge of the container once the pegs have been removed.

Containers, the inside of which will be lined, can be started from the base and worked upwards. When the knotting has reached the required length the cord-ends are glued to the inside of the container and concealed by the lining.

For bulbous containers, like vases or jars, work needs gradual opening out to allow for the increased circumference and is then brought back in again (see Colour Plate B).

119

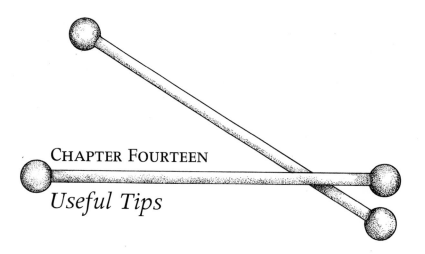

Chapter Fourteen

Useful Tips

Sewing cord-ends into the back of work
Some cord-ends are too thick to be sewn into the back of work successfully. It will help to unravel these into separate strands to be threaded in singly.

Pressing
Some knotting benefits from being pressed on the wrong side before sewing the individual sections together. Pieces which are slightly out of shape may be remedied by pinning these to the correct outlines and then pressing them. If any three-dimensional knots are part of the pattern pressing is not recommended.

Reversing cords when they are running short (Fig. 320)
Should certain Working Cords become rather short these may be reversed in suitable places to become Filler Cords. This is perhaps not entirely professional but may save an awkward situation. A good point for exchanging cords, especially in Sinnet patterns, is immediately after a corded line or wherever reversing is not too obvious. To reverse the cords of a Flat Knot bring the Filler Cords from the back under the Working Cords out to the left and right respectively. Now tie a Flat Knot using the previous Filler Cords as Working Cords. Push the knot up rather tightly and pull the Filler Cords down to hide the reversing. Sometimes it is necessary to reverse one short strand only. In this case just one cord is brought out to the side, reversing it with one of the Working Cords and leaving the remaining strands undisturbed (Fig. 320).

Inserting a piece of wood or a rod (Fig. 321)
Instead of working a complete row of Double Half Hitch Knots over a piece of wood, etc., it is

much quicker to form two loops in turn with each Working Cord, sliding these over the end of the rod. While obvious to some students others are not aware of this possibility. No cords need to be pulled through, thereby preserving the yarn.

Working rows of Cording with long strands (Fig. 322)
If you are working rows of either Horizontal or Diagonal Cording with very long strands, roll the Filler Cord into a ball, form two loops with each Working Cord in turn and push the ball through the loops. Tighten in the usual way. This is not only quicker but again preserves the yarn.

Working a Flat Knot pattern in two colours (Fig. 323)
When knotting a Flat Knot pattern in two colours, producing vertical stripes, an even pattern picture is only obtained by reversing certain Flat Knots (see drawing below). To reverse a Flat Knot see 'The Flat Knot' on page 22.

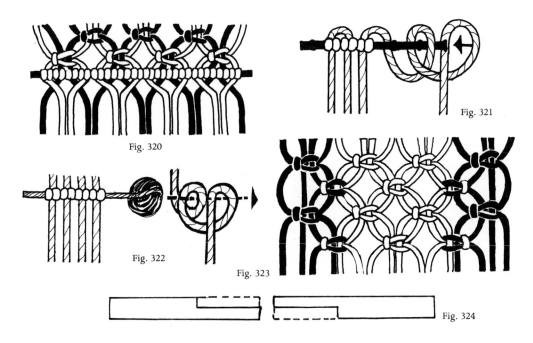

Fig. 320

Fig. 321

Fig. 322

Fig. 323

Fig. 324

Joining ends of basket cane (Fig. 324)
If basket cane is used as a base for working over, ends may be joined by splicing. Use a razor blade or sharp knife. Cut away half of the ends to be joined (about $\frac{1}{2}$ to 1 in ($1\frac{1}{2}$ to 2 cm) lengthways). Glue together and tie until set.

Coping with fraying ends
To stop cord-ends from fraying dip these lightly in fabric glue. Synthetic yarns may be singed. Cord-ends could also be knotted off with an Overhand Knot but this may cause excessive tangling.

To remedy bulging work
Particularly Sinnets are sometimes too long in relation to the rest of the knotting pattern. This causes bulging which can be remedied by threading a single strand through the back from top to bottom, at the same time drawing the work in gathering fashion. When adjusted to the right length knot off the end of the single cord and trim.

Starting with a fringe
Starting work with a fringe, as for instance on table mats, requires setting very tall Picots (see 'Picots' on page 47) onto a holding cord. These Picots are then cut open to form a fringe. The individual strands are knotted off with Overhand Knots, using two or four cords at a time. The ends may be unravelled into single strands to give a thicker but lighter fringe. If part of the fringe is to be knotted extra tall Picots are necessary to give adequate Working Cords. See Fig. 306 on page 112.

A further possibility to start work with a fringe is leaving a certain length from one end of a group of two or four cut strands before tying these together with an Overhand Knot. The Overhand Knots are then pinned next to each other and the Working Cords tied into Flat Knots (Fig. 325).

A longer strand could be included at either end to be taken across all other cords as Filler Cord for one or more rows of Horizontal Cording.

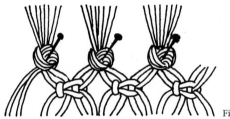
Fig. 325

Dyeing yarns
While the necessity for dyeing yarns has been inevitable in years past, this is not so today. An ever increasing choice of colours is available in many different kinds of yarn.

Some of the dyeing done by students has been very successful while in other cases the results have not always been perfect. Carefully follow the manufacturer's instructions and dye large enough quantities to avoid shade variations.

Do not despair if the end product of your dyeing is somewhat uneven and motley. We have worked with 'accidents of the trade' on many occasions in class and the result is, as a rule, unique in appearance and unexpectedly striking.

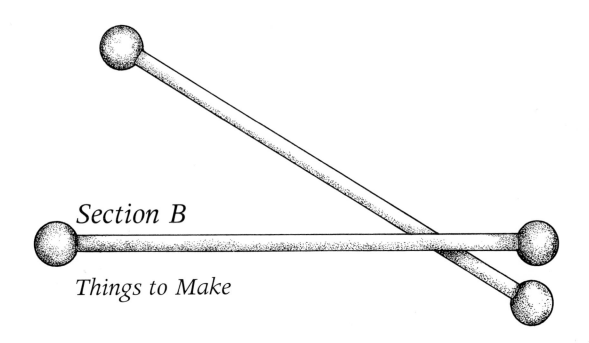

Section B

Things to Make

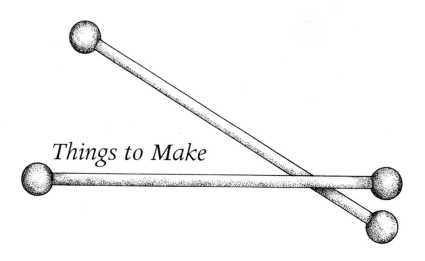

Things to Make

How to make a sampler (Fig. 326)

However tempted you may be to begin knotting with a project of particular appeal to you, I would always recommend making a sampler first. The learning pieces made in class always turn into very effective wall hangings, even if they are not perfect. Beginning with a sampler has the advantage of the knotter becoming familiar with various techniques and pattern possibilities straightaway. You will learn how to combine Sinnet patterns which can be worked to any length with more fabric-like textures of a definite size and shape. Practice to work in straight lines and to find the right knotting tension are two further opportunities a sampler provides. Students who, for one reason or another, have to join a course at a later stage and have not made a practice piece seldom reach the proficiency of those who have very quickly.

The sampler illustrated in Plate 39 is an example of a first piece of work made in class. The instructions for mounting cords do, as you will see, take into account the extra yarn required for the Working Cords of Sinnet Patterns and the Filler Cords for the dividing lines. Certain strands are set on unevenly and Fig. 326 should help you to do this successfully. Make sure that the cords, once set on, do not slip off the ends of the knot bearer.

As an alternative to the described sampler small individual trial pieces could be made up and then arranged on a background to form an unusual wall plaque.

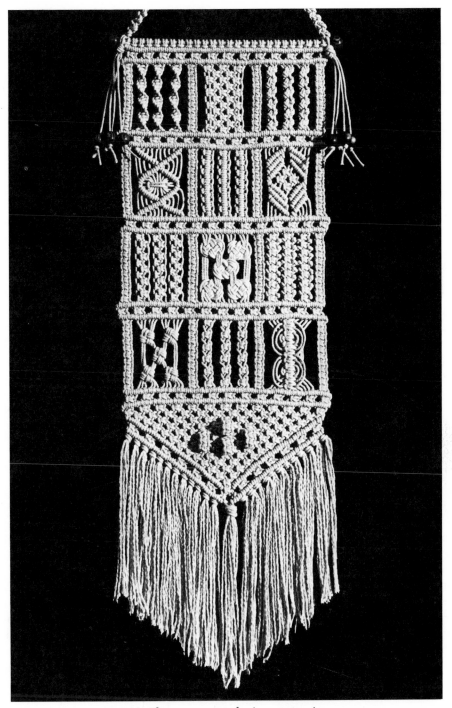

39 Elementary sampler in cotton twine

125

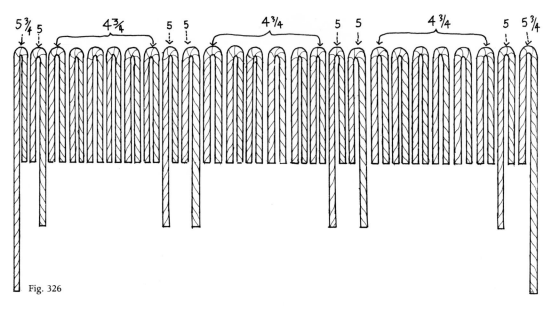

Fig. 326

Sampler

Size: 22 × 7½ in (19 × 55 cm).

MATERIAL Cotton twine or parcel string (about 1½–2 mm)
18 cords, each 4¾ yards (4.35 m) long
6 cords, each 5 yards (4.55 m) long
2 cords, each 5¾ yards (5.25 m) long
1 wooden stick or bamboo cane about 9 in (25 cm) long
2 beads

METHOD

1. Fold the eighteen 4¾-yard (4.35-m) cords in half and set onto the wooden stick with Lark's Head Knots (see 'Setting on Cords' on page 20).

2. Set the six 5-yard (4.55-m) cords onto the knot bearer as shown in the drawing above with one of the 5¾-yard (5.25-m) strands on the outside left and right respectively. Pin to board

3. Bring the cord on the outside left round a pin and place it horizontally over all remaining strands on the right. Using each cord in turn make a row of Horizontal Cording (see page 28) over it, starting from the left.

4. Using four cords at a time work a row of thirteen Flat Knots (see page 22), including the Filler Cord from the row of Cording in the last knot.

5. Bring the cord on the outside right round a pin and place it horizontally across all other strands on the left. Work a row of Horizontal Cording over it using each strand in turn, starting from the right.

6. With the first four cords on the outside left work a Flat Knot Sinnet (see page 33) eleven knots long, taking the Filler Cord from the row of Cording into the first knot.

7. Leave the next twelve cords unworked and make a second Flat Knot Sinnet eleven knots long with the next four strands on the right (17, 18, 19, 20).

8. Leave the next twelve cords unworked and make a third Flat Knot Sinnet eleven knots long with the next four strands on the right (33, 34, 35, 36).

9. Leave the next twelve cords unworked and make one more Flat Knot Sinnet eleven knots long with the four cords on the outside right.

You are now ready to work the first three pattern sections between the Flat Knot Sinnets. Start with the twelve cords in the centre.

Centre panel of first pattern section: Work eleven rows of Alternate Flat Knot pattern (see page 25), starting and ending with a row of three Flat Knots as follows: Using four cords at a time make three Flat Knots in the first row. Leaving out the first two and the last two strands tie two Flat Knots over the remaining eight cords. Repeat the first and second rows until eleven rows are completed. This section should now be the same length as the Sinnets on either side. Adjustments are possible by sliding the knotting of the Sinnets either up or down over the Filler Cords.

Left-hand panel of first pattern section: Using four cords at a time make three Banister Bars (see page 26) working these to the same length as the Sinnets on either side.

Right-hand panel of first pattern section: With two and two cords at a time work three Double Chains (see page 33) to the same length as the Sinnets on either side.

To work the dividing line between the first and second pattern sections: Bring the cord on the outside right round a pin and place it horizontally over all remaining strands on the left. Make a row of Horizontal Cording over it with each strand in turn, starting from the right. Using four cords at a time make a row of thirteen Flat Knots, taking the Filler Cord from the row of Cording into the first Flat Knot on the left. Bring the cord on the outside left round a pin and place it horizontally over all remaining strands on the right. Work a row of Horizontal Cording over it with each strand in turn, starting from the left (keep the Cording as straight as possible, using the lines on the board as a guide). To prepare the next pattern section work four Flat Knot Sinnets, each eleven knots long, as before.

Left-hand panel of second pattern section: Divide the twelve cords into two groups of six. Place the strand on the outside left from the left-hand group round a pin and diagonally over the next five strands on the right, sloping from left to right. Work a row of Diagonal Cording (see 'Diagonal Cording' on page 29) over it with each strand in turn, starting from the left. Bring the strand on the outside right from the right-hand group round a pin and diagonally across the five remaining strands on the left. Make a row of Diagonal Cording over it with each cord in turn, starting from the right.

To join the two diagonal lines the right-hand Filler Cord remains a Filler Cord and the left-hand Filler Cord becomes a Working Cord. Use the Working Cord to make one Double Half Hitch Knot over the Filler Cord. Place this same Filler Cord diagonally over the five strands on the left, sloping from right to left and make a row of Diagonal Cording over it with each strand in turn, starting from the right, continuing the diagonal line. Place the sixth cord from the right diagonally over the five strands on the right, sloping from left to right, and work a row of Diagonal Cording over it with each strand in turn, starting from the left. Leave out the Filler Cord on the outside left and right respectively and use the next strand from either side to make a Collective Flat Knot (see page 24) over all centre cords. Pin knot.

Bring the left-hand Filler Cord round a pin and place it diagonally over the next five strands on the right. Make a row of Diagonal Cording over it with each strand in turn, starting from the left. Bring the Filler Cord on the outside right round a pin and diagonally over the

127

five strands on the left. Make a row of Diagonal Cording over it with each strand in turn, starting from the right. Join the two Filler Cords as before by making one Double Half Hitch Knot with the left-hand one over the right. Place the Filler Cord diagonally over the five strands on the left and work a row of Diagonal Cording over it with each strand in turn, starting from the right. Place the sixth cord from the right diagonally over the five strands on the right and work a row of Diagonal Cording over it with each strand in turn, starting from the left. This pattern should be the same length as the Sinnets on either side. If not, adjust the Sinnets as described above.

Centre panel of second pattern section: Using four cords at a time work three Tatted Bars (see Sinnets on page 33) to the same length as the left-hand panel and Sinnets.

Right-hand panel of second pattern section: Divide the twelve cords into two groups of six. Bring the cord on the outside right of the left-hand group round a pin and place it diagonally over the five cords on the left, sloping from right to left. Work a row of Diagonal Cording over it with each strand in turn, starting from the right. Bring the next cord on the right (from the left-hand group) round a pin and diagonally over the five strands on the left. Work a second row of Diagonal Cording over it, immediately below the first one, using each strand in turn, starting from the right and taking in the Filler Cord from the previous row of Cording. With the next cord on the right (from the left-hand group) as Filler Cord, work a third row of Diagonal Cording similar to the second.

Bring the cord on the outside left of the right-hand group round a pin and place it diagonally over the five strands on the right. Using each strand in turn, work a row of Diagonal Cording over it, starting from the left. Make two more rows of Diagonal Cording to match the left-hand side. Find the centre four cords, two from the right and two from the left-hand group respectively and tie one Flat Knot over four cords. With the two left-hand cords from that Flat Knot and the next two cords on the left work one Flat Knot. With the two right-hand cords from the centre Flat Knot and the next two cords on the right make another Flat Knot. Work one more Flat Knot over the four centre strands. Bring the Filler Cord on the outside left round a pin and place it diagonally over the next five strands on the right, sloping from left to right. Make a row of Diagonal Cording over it with each strand in turn, starting from the left. Bring the next cord from the outside left round a pin and place it diagonally over the five strands on the right. Make a second row of Diagonal Cording over it with each strand in turn, starting from the left and taking in the Filler Cord from the previous row of Cording. Bring the next cord from the outside left round a pin and work a third row of Diagonal Cording over it similar to the second.

Bring the Filler Cord on the outside right round a pin and place it diagonally over the five strands on the left, sloping from right to left. Make a row of Diagonal Cording over it with each strand in turn, starting from the right. Bring the next cord on the outside right round a pin and place it diagonally over the five strands on the left. Make a second row of Diagonal Cording over it with each strand in turn, starting from the right, taking in the Filler Cord from the previous row of Cording. Bring the next cord on the outside right round a pin and work a third row of Diagonal Cording over it similar to the second.

Knot the next dividing line between the second and third pattern sections using the cord on the outside left as Filler Cord for the first row of Horizontal Cording. Make a row of thirteen Flat Knots, then bring back the cord on the outside right as Filler Cord for the second row of Horizontal Cording.

128

To prepare the third pattern section make four Flat Knot Sinnets eleven knots long, as before.

Left-hand panel of third pattern section: Using four cords at a time knot three Alternate Flat Knot Braids as follows: with the three cords on the outside left make one Flat Knot, using one Filler Cord only. Leaving the cord on the outside left unworked tie a Flat Knot with the next three cords on the right. Keep making Flat Knots with the left-hand three and then the right-hand three strands. Work all three braids to the same length as the Sinnets on either side (see page 39).

Centre panel of third pattern section: Divide the twelve cords into two groups of six. Take three and three strands from the group on the left and work one Josephine Knot (see page 40). Repeat with the six cords from the right-hand group. Using three strands from the left and three cords from the right-hand Josephine Knot work a further Josephine Knot in the centre. With the three cords from the left of this Josephine Knot and the three cords on the outside left work another Josephine Knot and similarly with the remaining six cords on the right. Position the knots in such a way that the arrangement is similar to that in the photograph on page 125.

Right-hand panel of third pattern section: Using four cords at a time make three Flat Knot Sinnets with Overhand Knot Side Picots (see 'Sinnets' on page 35) and adjust these to the same length as the previous work in this section.

For the dividing line between the third and fourth pattern sections use the cord on the outside right as Filler Cord for the first row of Horizontal Cording. Work a row of thirteen Flat Knots and use the cord on the outside left as Filler Cord for the second row of Horizontal Cording.

Prepare the fourth pattern section by making four Flat Knot Sinnets eleven knots long, as before.

Left-hand panel of fourth pattern section: Divide the twelve cords into two groups of six. Using three and three strands from the left-hand group work one Chinese Crown Knot (see page 41). Repeat with the six cords from the group on the right. Taking three strands from the knot on the left and three from the right-hand one make one Chinese Crown Knot in the centre. With the three left-hand cords from this knot and the three strands on the outside left work another Chinese Crown Knot and similarly with the three right-hand cords from the Chinese Crown Knot in the centre and the three strands on the outside right. The arrangement of the five knots should be similar to that in the photograph on page 125.

Centre panel of fourth pattern section: Using four cords at a time work three Sinnets 'Variation on Flat Knot Sinnet' (see 'Sinnets' on page 34) and adjust the length to the Flat Knot Sinnets on either side.

Right-hand panel of fourth pattern section: The technique for this circular pattern is described under 'Special effects—Technique based on Flat Knot' see page 81. The knotting in the sampler is done over four Filler Cords, leaving four Working Cords on either side. The working procedure remains the same but the number of graduating circles will be reduced to three for the pattern to fit into the available space. Knot two shapes and pin frequently.

To make the last dividing line between the fourth section and the point use the cord on the outside left as Filler Cord for the first row of Horizontal Cording. Make a row of thirteen Flat Knots and bring back the strand on the outside right as Filler Cord for the second row of Horizontal Cording.

129

Working the point: (Fig. 327)

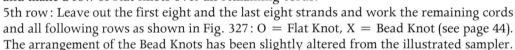

5th row→

Fig. 327

1st row: Make a row of Flat Knots over all strands, using four cords at a time.

2nd row: Leave out the first two and the last two strands and make a row of Flat Knots over all remaining cords.

3rd: Leave out the first four and the last four strands and make a row of Flat Knots over all remaining cords.

4th row: Leave out the first six and the last six strands and make a row of Flat Knots over all remaining cords.

5th row: Leave out the first eight and the last eight strands and work the remaining cords and all following rows as shown in Fig. 327: O = Flat Knot, X = Bead Knot (see page 44).

The arrangement of the Bead Knots has been slightly altered from the illustrated sampler.

Bring the cord on the outside left round a pin and diagonally along the side of the pointed section as Filler Cord. Make a row of Diagonal Cording over it with each cord in turn, starting from the left and including the left-hand Working Cord from the single Flat Knot at the centre point. Work the right-hand side to match. Use the Filler Cords from the Diagonal Cording on the left and right respectively as Working Cords to make one Flat Knot over the two Filler Cords from the Flat Knot at the centre point.

Starting from the outside left and using four cords at a time tie six Flat Knots along the side edge of the pointed section. Work the right-hand side to match. With the two left-hand cords from the centre Flat Knot work a Single Chain (see page 33) of two knots only and repeat with the two right-hand strands.

Bring the cord on the outside left round a pin and place it diagonally over all strands from the Flat Knots on the left. Make a row of Diagonal Cording over it with each strand in turn, starting from the left and including the two cords from the left-hand Single Chain. Work right-hand side to match.

To finish: Make one Overhand Knot (see page 35) with the four centre strands. Starting from the outside left and using two cords at a time make twelve Overhand Knots along the left edge and work the right-hand side to match . Cut the cord-ends either to a point or in a straight horizontal line. Trim the ends with beads, if wished, or unravel each cord into separate strands as on the illustrated sampler. Slip one bead over each end of the knot bearer and hold in place with a little glue if necessary.

Keyrings

KEYRING 1

MATERIAL   Coloured cotton twine ($1\frac{1}{2}$ mm) or parcel string   1 keyring

2 cords, each 1 yard (90 cm) long   1 medium size bead

METHOD

1. Fold each 1-yard (90-cm) cord in half and, in turn, set onto the keyring with Lark's Head Knots (see page 20).

2. Using two and two cord-ends tie about five Josephine Knots (see page 40), one below the other. **Important:** the Josephine Knots must be tied alternately, one from the left and the next from the right, in order to prevent the work from twisting.

3. Thread one bead over all four cord-ends, hold in place with an Overhand Knot (see page 35) and leave about 1 in (2½ cm) before trimming ends.

KEYRING 2

MATERIAL   Coloured cotton twine (1½ mm) or   1 keyring
            parcel string   15 small beads
            2 cords, each 1 yard (90 cm) long

METHOD
1. Fold each 1-yard (90-cm) cord in half and, in turn, set onto the keyring with Lark's Head Knots (see page 20). Pin to board.
2. *Using the three left-hand strands first work one Flat Knot (see page 22) (one Filler Cord only). Thread one bead over the end of the fourth cord and push up against the Lark's Head Knot.
3. With the three right-hand strands tie one Flat Knot (one Filler Cord only). Thread one bead over the end of the strand on the outside left and move it up to the first Flat Knot.
4. Repeat from * four more times then work 2. once more. Knot off two cord-ends at a time with one Overhand Knot (see page 35).
5. Thread one bead onto each single cord-end and knot off with an Overhand Knot to hold in place. Trim ends.

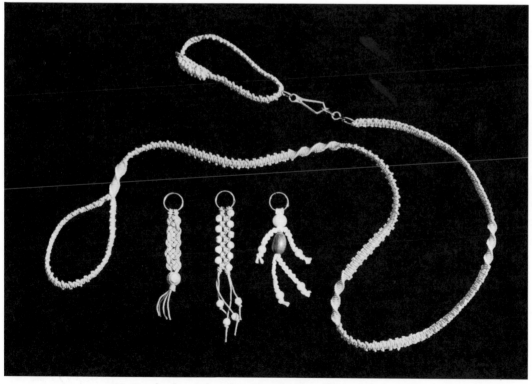

40 Dog lead and three keyrings (numbered from left to right)

131

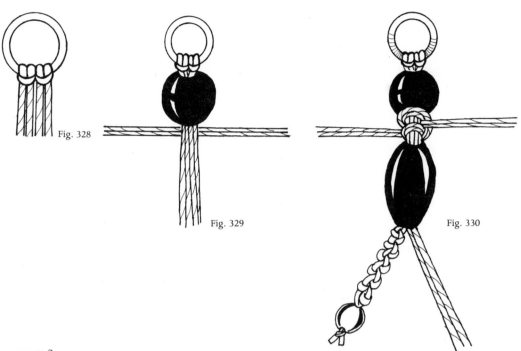

Fig. 328

Fig. 329

Fig. 330

KEYRING 3

MATERIAL Parcel string (2 mm)
                2 cords, each 32 in (80 cm) long
                2 cords, each 30 in (75 cm) long
                1 keyring

1 round bead, about $\frac{5}{8}$ in ($1\frac{3}{4}$ cm) diameter
1 oval bead, about 1 in ($2\frac{1}{2}$ cm) long
4 small beads

METHOD
1. Fold each 32-in (80-cm) cord in half and set onto the keyring, in turn, with Lark's Head Knots (Fig. 328).
2. Thread the round $\frac{5}{8}$-in ($1\frac{3}{4}$-cm) bead over all four cord-ends and move up to the Lark's Head Knots (Fig. 329).
3. Take two of the 30-in (75-cm) cords, place these together and position the midway point under the four cords, just below the bead, with the ends horizontally out to the left and right respectively. Pin the two ends on the right-hand side of the four centre cords. With the two left-hand ends make one Double Half Hitch Knot (see page 28) over the four cords coming from the bead to form the neck.
4. Thread the oval bead over the four cord-ends and move up to the neck.
5. Using two cord-ends at a time (from the bead) make two Single Chains (see page 33) about 2 in (5 cm) long to form the legs (Fig. 330). Thread one small bead over the two ends from each Single Chain and hold in place with Overhand Knots (see page 35). Trim ends, leaving small tassels.
6. On either side of the neck work a Single Chain about $1\frac{1}{4}$ in ($3\frac{1}{4}$ cm) long for the arms. Again slip a small bead over two ends at a time, hold in place with Overhand Knots, then trim, leaving small tassels.

White choker with coloured beads

(Plate 48 on page 172, reverse side shown)

MATERIAL   White tubular rayon   About 12 beads
            6 cords, each $1\frac{1}{4}$ yards (1.15 m) long   Neck measurement 13 in (33 cm),
            4 cords, each $3\frac{3}{4}$ yards (3.45 m) long   (work longer or shorter as required)

METHOD

1. Take two long and two short strands, place four ends together and leaving 14 in (35 cm) unworked tie a temporary Overhand Knot (see page 35) over all four strands. (Fig. 331). Pin this knot to the board, long ends down, and arrange the four cords in such a way that the two shorter ones are in the centre and the longer ones on either side. Work a Flat Knot Sinnet (see page 33) seven knots long with the two outside Working Cords.

2. Place two $1\frac{1}{4}$-yard (1.15-m) cords together, measure 14 in (35 cm) from one end and tie a temporary Overhand Knot over both strands. Pin this knot to the right of the previous Overhand Knot with long ends down.

3. Work as 1. but pin the Overhand Knot to the right of the two previous ones. You should now have two Flat Knot Sinnets, each seven knots long, with two single strands running down the centre.

4. Thread one bead onto the two centre cords and move it up between the Sinnets. Cross the right-hand Sinnet over the left (Fig. 332).

5. Using a needle thread each of the two single cords from the bead in turn through the top and then the bottom of the cross-over, at the back of work, thereby holding the overlapping Sinnets in place. Leave the two strands to run down the centre again (Fig. 333).

6. Make another seven Flat Knots on each Sinnet, thread one bead over the centre cords, then cross the Sinnets again, right over left, as before.

7. Continue in this way until ten beads have been inserted. Do not cross the Sinnets after the tenth bead.

8. Bring the cord on the outside right from the left-hand Sinnet diagonally over the four strands from the right-hand Sinnet and using each cord in turn, make a row of Diagonal Cording (see page 29) over it, starting from the left. From this corded line take the strand on the outside left and place it diagonally over the three remaining cords from the Flat Knot Sinnet on the left. Using each of the three cords in turn work a row of Diagonal Cording over it, starting from the right. Place the first cord on the right from this last row of Cording diagonally over the three strands on the right and work a row of Diagonal Cording over it with each strand in turn, starting from the left and leaving out the previous Filler Cord. Bring the left-hand cord from this last row of Cording over the two strands on the left and make two Double Half Hitch Knots over it with each cord in turn, leaving out the previous Filler Cord. Place the right-hand cord from this last row of Cording over the two strands on the right and work two Double Half Hitch Knots over it with each strand in turn, leaving out the previous Filler Cord. Bring the left-hand cord from these two knots diagonally over the remaining strand on the left and make one Double Half Hitch Knot (see page 29) over it, leaving out the previous Filler Cord. Place the cord from this Double Half Hitch Knot diagonally over the remaining strand on the right and work a further Double Half Hitch Knot. (Fig. 334)

133

9. Bring the first Filler Cord on the outside left round a pin and diagonally along the edge of the Cording. Using each strand in turn work a row of Diagonal Cording (three knots) over it, starting from the left. Work right-hand side to match, thereby bringing the work to a point (Fig. 334).
10. Tie the two Filler Cords at the point together with one Overhand Knot and sew the remaining cord-ends into the back of work.
11. About 12 in (30 cm) from the Overhand Knot thread a bead over both strands, hold in place with an Overhand Knot and trim. Untie the three temporary Overhand Knots at the other end and work from 8. for the two ends to match.

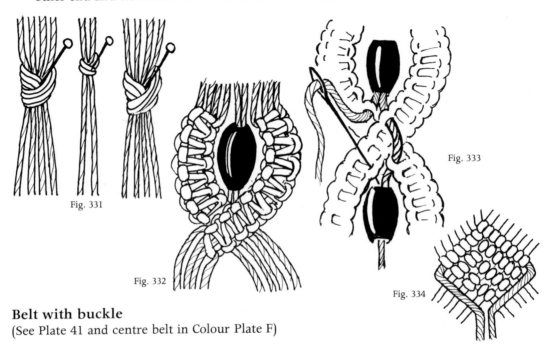

Fig. 331

Fig. 332

Fig. 333

Fig. 334

Belt with buckle
(See Plate 41 and centre belt in Colour Plate F)

MATERIAL   Cotton twine ($1\frac{1}{2}$–2 mm)
             8 Cords, each $11\frac{1}{2}$ yards (10.45 m) long, for a 26-in (65-cm) waist
    or   8 cords, each 11 yards (10 m) long, for a 24-in (60-cm) waist
             1 buckle with a 2-in (5-cm) bar
For loop: 1 cord, 2 yards (1.80 m) long
             1 cord, 24 in (60 cm) long

METHOD
1. Fold each cord in half and mount onto the cross bar of the buckle with Lark's Head Knots (see page 20).
2. Using four cords at a time work four Flat Knots (see page 22). *Leaving out the first two and the last two strands make three Flat Knots over the remaining twelve cords. Leaving out the first four and the last four cords work two Flat Knots with the remaining eight strands.

134

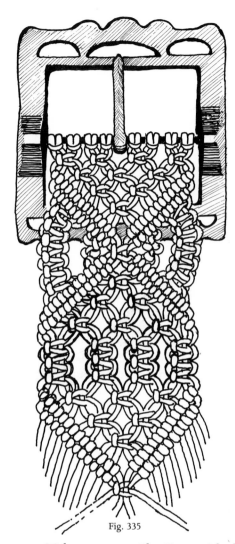

Fig. 335

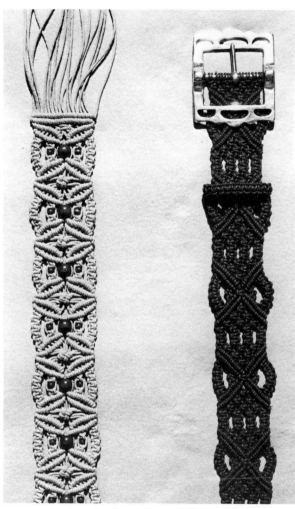

41 Details of tie belt and belt with clasp

Make one more Flat Knot with the four centre cords, thereby bringing this Flat Knot section to a point. Use Fig. 335 as a working diagram.

3. Bring the cord on the outside left round a pin and diagonally, as Filler Cord, along the left-hand edge of the Flat Knot section. Using each of the next seven cords on the right in turn, make a row of Diagonal Cording (see page 29), starting from the left.

4. Bring the next strand on the outside left round a pin and diagonally over the next six cords on the right as second Filler Cord. Using each of the six cords in turn work a second row of Diagonal Cording immediately below the previous one, starting from the left.

5. Work right-hand side to match.

6. With the four Filler Cords in the centre make one Flat Knot. With the next two strands on the left knot a Single Chain (see page 33) four knots long. Using the four cords on the outside left work a Flat Knot Sinnet (see page 33) six knots long.

Knot the right-hand side to match.

7. Pin the Flat Knot in the centre and bring the left-hand Working Cord from that knot diagonally over the next six strands on the left (two from the Single Chain and four from the Flat Knot Sinnet). Using each of these six cords in turn work a row of Diagonal Cording over the Filler Cord, starting from the right.

8. Place the left-hand Filler Cord from the Flat Knot diagonally over the seven strands on the left and knot a second row of Diagonal Cording over it with each strand in turn, starting from the right. Work right-hand side to match.

9. With the four centre cords make one Flat Knot.
   Using the two left-hand cords from that Flat Knot and the next two strands on the left work a second Flat Knot. Similarly, tie a Flat Knot with the two right-hand cords from the first Flat Knot and the next two strands on the right.
   Work one Flat Knot with the four centre cords and one each on the left and right of this knot.
   Using four cords at a time and starting from the outside left, work four Flat Knot Sinnets, each three knots long. Repeat this pattern from * as often as required, ending with a point of three, two and then one Flat Knot.

10. Work the corded edge as before but join the first two diagonal rows of Cording in the centre by making one Double Half Hitch Knot (see page 28) with the right-hand Filler Cord over the left. Starting with the cord on the outside right as Filler Cord for the second row of Cording, include the Filler Cord from the joining knot at the end. Work the second row of Diagonal Cording from the left in the opposite way, again including the Filler Cord from the Cording on the right at the end. Cut all cords about $\frac{1}{2}$ in ($1\frac{1}{4}$ cm) from the Cording, apply some fabric glue along the edge of the point at the back of work and pin all ends down until dry.

To work the loop:
Fold the 2-yard (1.80-m) cord in half and pin the loop to the board with the cord-ends in a downward direction. Fold the 24-in (60-cm) cord in half and pin the loop immediately below and inside the previous one.

Using the two longer ends on the outside left and right respectively as Working Cords make a Flat Knot Sinnet about twenty-two knots long. Push the two Filler Cords through the loops at the beginning of the Sinnet with a needle. Turn the looped Sinnet inside out and sew the two Filler Cords in one direction and the two Working Cords in the other into the back of work. Turn the loop back on right side and slip over the end of the belt, moving it along to the right position (see page 106, Figs. 277–279).

Tie belt with beads
(Plate 41 on page 135 and Colour Plate F)

MATERIAL	Cotton twine ($1\frac{1}{2}$–2 mm)
	16 cords, each 5 yards (4.55 m) long (max. 26-in (65-cm) waist. Cut longer cords if larger belt is required)
For belt:	12–14 beads, $\frac{3}{8}$–$\frac{1}{2}$ in (1–$1\frac{1}{4}$ cm) diameter (number varies according to size waist)
	24–28 small beads

For tie

ends: 12 beads, $\frac{3}{8}$–$\frac{1}{2}$ in (1–1$\frac{1}{4}$ cm) diameter

        40 small beads

        (As an alternative the tie ends could be trimmed with Coil Knots)

METHOD

1. Place the sixteen strands together and measuring about 14 in (35 cm) from one end tie all cords together with a temporary Overhand Knot (see page 35). Pin this knot to the board with the long cord-ends down. Bring the cord on the outside left round a pin and place it horizontally over all remaining strands on the right. Using each cord in turn work a row of Horizontal Cording (see page 28) over it, starting from the left. Bring the same Filler Cord round a pin and back over the remaining strands as Filler Cord for the second row of Horizontal Cording, using each cord in turn and starting from the right. Use Fig. 336 as a working diagram.

2. Work a Collective Flat Knot (see page 24) over the six centre strands, using the cord on either side as Working Cords with four Filler Cords.

3. *Bring the Filler Cord on the outside left round a pin and work the top half of a leaf shape with each of the next seven cords in turn, starting from the left (see 'Leaf Shapes' on page 29). Using the next strand on the left as Filler Cord knot the lower edge of the leaf.

4. Work one complete leaf shape with the eight cords on the right, using the strand on the outside right as the first Filler Cord, and knotting in the opposite direction.

5. Thread one of the larger beads onto the two centre strands, thereby joining the two leaves together.

6. Leave one cord on either side of the bead unworked. Make a Flat Knot with the next three strands (using one Filler Cord only) on either side. Slip a small bead over the ends of the single Filler Cords and push up against the Flat Knots. Hold in place with a second Flat Knot over three strands.

7. With the three remaining cords on the outside left and right respectively work two Flat Knot Sinnets (see page 33), each five knots long, using one Filler Cord only.

8. The cords taken through the large bead now in turn become the Filler Cords for the top edges of the next leaf shapes. Using the left-hand one first, bring it round a pin and place over the seven strands on the left. Starting the Cording from the right, take in first the unworked cord next to the bead, then the three strands from the small bead section and finally the three cords from the Flat Knot Sinnet on the outside left. Using the next cord from the right as Filler Cord knot the lower edge of the leaf, starting from the right.

9. Work a complete leaf shape with the eight cords on the right, starting with the strand from the large bead as first Filler Cord and knotting in the opposite direction.

10. Using the fourth and fifth strands from each leaf pattern make a Chinese Crown Knot (see 'Chinese Crown Knot' on page 41), leaving all other cords straight and unworked.

11. Repeat from * as often as necessary until the required length belt is reached (make certain that the cords from the Chinese Crown Knot are brought back into the pattern in their right order).

12. To match the two ends of the belt work a Collective Flat Knot over the six centre cords immediately after the last leaves and omit the Chinese Crown Knot.

13. Bring the cord on the outside left round a pin and place it horizontally over all remaining

137

strands from left to right. Using each cord in turn make a row of Horizontal Cording over it, starting from the left. Bring back the same Filler Cord, round a pin, and place it horizontally over all remaining strands on the left. Work a row of Horizontal Cording over it with each strand in turn, starting from the right.

14. Tie an Overhand Knot with the end of the Filler Cord, move it up to hold the Cording in place and tighten.

15. Undo the temporary Overhand Knot at the beginning of work and tie the first Filler Cord in the same way. Trim the cord-ends at the end of the belt to the same length as those at the beginning.

16. At each end of the belt thread a large bead onto the first cord on the outside left, two small ones each onto the second and third strands, one large bead onto the fourth, two small ones each onto the fifth and sixth cords, etc. Hold all beads in place with Overhand Knots then trim ends.

Fig. 337

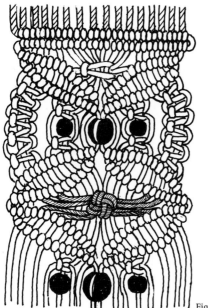

Fig. 336

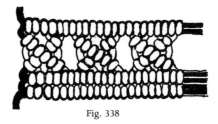

Fig. 338

Bag with patterned handles
Finished size: $8\frac{1}{2} \times 9\frac{1}{2}$ in (22 × 24 cm)

MATERIAL	Cotton twine ($1\frac{1}{2}$-2 m)
For Bag:	2 cords, each $6\frac{1}{2}$ yards (5.90 m) long
	36 cords, each 6 yards (5.50 m) long
	2 cords, each 28 in (71 cm) long, for sewing sides together
For Handles:	4 cords, each 16 yards (14.60 m) long
	2 cords, each 23 yards (21 m) long

138

METHOD

Bag:

1. Place the two 6½-yard (5.90-m) cords together, fold these in half and pin the midway points to the board. Measure 4¾ in (12 cm) horizontally to the left and then to the right of the pins and secure both cords again at these points. The two strands now form a double holding cord.
2. Remove the centre pins and set on the thirty-six cords measuring 6 yards (5.50 m) between the pinned points with Lark's Head Knots (see page 20). Pin in a straight horizontal line.
3. Starting from the left and using four cords at a time work alternate rows of Flat Knots (see 'Alternate Flat Knot Pattern' on page 25) until the knotting measures 21 in (54 cm).
4. Place the cords on the outside left and right respectively against and over each other to form a double Filler Cord (Fig. 337). Starting from the left and using each strand in turn make a row of Horizontal Cording (see page 28) over both cords. Pull the ends of the Filler Cords out to the left and right respectively to tighten.
5. Place the cord on the outside left as Filler Cord diagonally over the second strand, sloping from left to right, and make one Double Half Hitch Knot (see page 28) with the second strand over the first. Bring the fourth cord from the left diagonally over the third, sloping from right to left, and make one Double Half Hitch Knot with the third strand over the fourth (Fig. 338).
6. The right-hand Filler Cord now becomes a Working Cord. Use this to make one Double Half Hitch Knot over the left-hand Filler Cord, keeping the line diagonal. Place the second cord from the left diagonally over the first, sloping from right to left and make one Double Half Hitch Knot with the first strand over the second.
7. Using four cords at a time repeat this diagonal cross pattern (5. and 6.) right across the line.
8. Place the cord on the outside left and right respectively against and over each other to form a Double Filler Cord (Fig. 337). Using each strand in turn work a row of Horizontal Cording over these, starting from the left. Pull the ends of the Filler Cords out to the left and right respectively to tighten.
9. Repeat 8.
10. Cut all ends about ½ in (1¼ cm) below the last row of Cording and glue to the back of work. Pin each strand to hold in place until dry.
11. Line the knotted rectangle with lining material or felt, leaving the side loops formed by the Alternate Flat Knot Pattern free.
12. On one side count nineteen side loops from the Lark's Head Knot end of the work and fold the knotting at this point to form pocket. Match up with the next nineteen side loops and pin. Repeat on the other side.
13. With a needle bring one of the 28-in (71-cm) cords through the two top loops and pull ends even. Oversew once through both top loops, then join the back and the front section by making running stitches through the matched up loops, first with one end of the sewing thread from the front and then with the other from the back (see page 64). Repeat on the other side. Turn the bag inside out and knot off the ends of the sewing threads. Dab a little glue to make more secure. When the adhesive is completely dry turn the bag back onto the right side.

42 Handbag with patterned handles in cotton twine

To work handles: The handles consist of one long knotted strap 68 in (1.73 m) long and can be worked in any pattern of your choice. This may be desirable to give the bag an individual look. The method for the pictured handles is as follows:

1. Fold one of the 16-yard (14.60-m) cords in half and pin the midway point to the board. Measure about 1 in (2.5 cm) horizontally to the left and right of this pin and secure the cord with a pin in both places (holding cord).

2. Remove the centre pin. Fold the remaining three 16-yard (14.60-m) cords in half and mount along the centre of the holding cord with Lark's Head Knots. Fold the two 23-yard (21-m) strands in such a way that one end measures 8 yards (7.20 m) and the other 15 yards (13.65 m). Mount one to the left and one to the right of the already set on cords with the shorter ends towards the centre and the longer ones on the outside. The two ends of the holding cord are now taken into the work and should be on the outside left and right respectively.

3. Counting from the left use the cords 3, 4, 5 and 6 to make one Double Crossed Knot (see page 28). Repeat with the next four strands on the right (7, 8, 9 and 10). Make one more Double Crossed Knot with the four centre strands (two right-hand strands from the first Double Crossed Knot and two left-hand strands from the second immediately above).

4. Bring the cord on the outside left round a pin and place it diagonally over the next five strands on the right, sloping from left to right. Using each cord in turn, make a row of Diagonal Cording (see page 29) over it, starting from the left. Bring the cord on the outside right round a pin and place it diagonally over the next five strands on the left, sloping from right to left. Using each cord in turn make a row of Diagonal Cording over it, starting from the right.

5. Bring the cord on the outside left round a pin and use it as Working Cord to tie a Vertical Double Half Hitch Knot (see 'Vertical Cording' on page 31) over each of the next five strands on the right, following the diagonal line provided by the row of Cording above. Anchor the next cord on the left with a pin and place it as Filler Cord diagonally over the next five strands on the right. Using each cord in turn make a row of Diagonal Cording over it, starting from the left.

6. Work the right-hand six cords to match, starting with the cord on the outside right as Working Cord to make Vertical Double Half Hitch Knots over the next five strands on the left.

7. Now join the two rows of Diagonal Cording. For this purpose the Filler Cord from the left-hand row remains a Filler Cord and the one from the right becomes a Working Cord. Use the right-hand one to make a Double Half Hitch Knot over the left-hand strand.

8. Place the last Filler Cord horizontally over the five strands on the right and using each cord in turn work a row of Horizontal Cording, starting from the left. Bring the same Filler Cord back, round a pin, and over the next five strands on the left. Work a second row of Horizontal Cording over it, immediately below the previous one and using each strand in turn, starting from the right. Work the left-hand six cords to match, using the cord on the right of that group as Filler Cord.

9. To join the two rows of Horizontal Cording the Filler Cord from the left remains a Filler Cord and the one from the right becomes a Working Cord. Tie one Double Half Hitch Knot with the right-hand one over the left (use Fig. 339 as working diagram).

10. Still using the same Filler Cord place this diagonally over the next five strands on the right, sloping from left to right, and with each one in turn make a row of Diagonal Cording over it, starting from the left.

11. Bring the sixth cord from the outside left round a pin and place it diagonally over the next five strands on the left, sloping from right to left. Work a row of Diagonal Cording over it, using each strand in turn and starting from the right.

12. With the cord on the outside right from the left-hand group of six strands as Working Cord tie one Vertical Double Half Hitch Knot over each of the next five strands on the left. Bring the next cord on the right from this group round a pin and place it diagonally over the next five strands on the left. Using each cord in turn work a row of Diagonal Cording over it, starting from the right.

13. Work the right-hand group of six cords to match, using the strand on the outside left as Working Cord for the line of Vertical Double Half Hitch Knots.

14. Tie a Double Crossed Knot with the four centre strands (two from the left-hand group and two from the right). Repeat the pattern from 3. twenty-five more times.

15. To join the two ends of the strap push the cord-ends in turn from the right side through the spaces below the holding cord and knot two and two together on the reverse side.

16. Place the join along the base of the bag, about 1½ in (3¾ cm) from the side edge on the

right. Push the cord-ends through to the inside of the bag, using a needle, and knot off again, thereby attaching the strap. Place the fold of the strap along the base of the bag on the opposite side, about $1\frac{1}{2}$ in ($3\frac{3}{4}$ cm) from the side edge on the left. Make certain that the pattern picture matches that on the right. Use a piece of extra cord to attach the fold to the base of the bag and knot off end on the inside. Now secure the strap in a similar way to the front of the bag. This is done higher up at the sides of the next Double Crossed Knot pattern. Repeat on right-hand side.

17. Turn the bag over and, using extra strands, attach the strap at the sides of the first Double Crossed Knot patterns from the top edge.

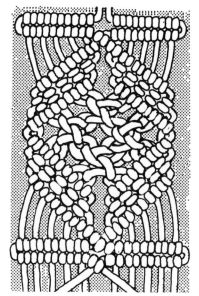

Simple plant hanger
Fig. 339

(Plate 43 on page 145)
Finished length including tassels: 45 in (1.15 m)

MATERIAL

Coloured sisal ($2\frac{1}{2}$–3 mm)
4 cords, each $4\frac{1}{2}$ yards (4.10 m) long
1 wooden curtain ring 2–$2\frac{1}{2}$ in (5–6 cm) diameter

4 cords, each $8\frac{1}{2}$ yards (7.75 m) long
32 small beads with fairly large holes
8 oval beads

METHOD

1. Place the four shorter cords together and push one end through the wooden ring pulling all ends even. Place the four longer strands together, push one end through the ring and arrange over the already positioned cords, pulling the ends of the longer cords even (Fig. 340).

2. Find the two ends from one of the longer cords on the outside right and left respectively and use these as double Working Cords to make eight Flat Knots (see page 22), one below the other, over the remaining strands in the centre (Fig. 341).

142

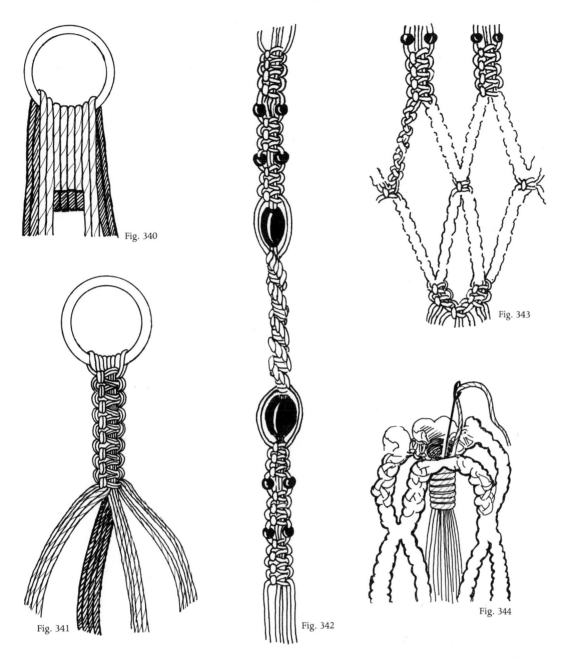

Fig. 340

Fig. 341

Fig. 342

Fig. 343

Fig. 344

3. Divide the sixteen cords into four groups of four strands, two long ends and two short ones in each set.

4. Working with one group first, use the longer strands as Working Cords and make a Flat Knot Sinnet (see page 33) sixteen knots long over the two Filler Cords. Repeat with the remaining three sets of four strands. (The thickness of sisal is not always constant and it

143

is necessary to check that all four Sinnets are the same length. The variation in the yarn can result in longer or shorter Sinnets and this has to be counteracted by pushing the Flat Knots either up or down over the Filler Cords. Alternatively, an extra knot could be worked or one left out.)

5. *Thread one small bead onto each of the Working Cords from one Sinnet then tie three Flat Knots (Fig. 342), using the same Working Cords. Repeat from *.
6. Thread one oval bead over the two Filler Cords and move up against the last Flat Knot. Still using the same Working Cords make a Banister Bar (see page 26) twisting five times.
7. Thread another oval bead over the Filler Cords, move it up against the spiral and ** still using the same Working Cords tie three Flat Knots over the two Filler Cords.
8. Thread one small bead onto each of the two Working Cords and move up. Repeat from **.
9. Work another Flat Knot Sinnet twenty knots long; then knot the three remaining groups of cords to this point (check that the length of each individual section is identical).
10. Divide the four cords from each Flat Knot Sinnet into two groups of two strands (Fig. 343). With each set of two cords make a Single Chain (see page 33) about twenty-two knots long.
11. Place the right-hand Single Chain from one Sinnet and the left-hand one from the next on the right together and use the two outside cords to make one Flat Knot over the two centre strands (make certain that the Sinnets are in their right order and not twisted). Repeat 11. three more times, right round the work.
12. Again divide the four cords from each Flat Knot into two groups of two strands and in turn work a Single Chain of about twenty knots with each set.
13. Finally, place the right-hand Single Chain from one Flat Knot and the left-hand one from the next on the right together and use the two outside strands to make two Flat Knots one below the other over the two centre cords. Repeat 13. three more times right round the work. Tie four more Flat Knots using two strands from one and two cords from the next group of two Flat Knots, right round the work.
14. Find the longest cord-end and wrap it round all remaining strands, working down (Fig. 344). When eight to ten wrappings have been completed push the end of this cord up through the centre, using a needle, and sew it through the work in several places, along the inside of the base, before bringing it down through the centre again to form part of the tassel. Pull all ends down to give a neat tassel, then trim to the required length.

Large jute plant hanger
(Colour Plate G)
Finished length: 6 ft 10 in (2.05 m) with a bowl of 14 in (36 cm) diameter

MATERIAL   Thick jute (7 mm)   2 wooden rings, $3\frac{3}{4}$ in (10 cm)
            12 cords, each $15\frac{1}{2}$ yards (14.10 m)   diameter
            long   4 large wooden beads, $2 \times 1\frac{1}{2}$ in
            1 wooden curtain ring, $2\frac{3}{4}$ in (7 cm) $(5 \times 3\frac{3}{4}$ cm) diameter
            diameter

METHOD
1. Place the cords together, push one end through the curtain ring, pulling ends even.

2. Using the two ends from one cord on the outside left and right respectively as double Working Cords tie a Banister Bar about seven knots long (see page 26) over the remaining strands (Fig. 345).

3. Divide the twenty-four strands into four groups of six cords and tie nine Crown Knots (see 'Crown Knot' on page 00), one on top of another.

4. Push one of the larger wooden rings over all cord-ends and move it up to the Crown Knot Section (Fig. 346). From below work one Double Half Hitch Knot (see page 28) with each strand in turn over the ring to cover completely.

5. Divide the twenty-four strands into four groups of six. Tie the cords of each of three groups together with a temporary Overhand Knot (see 'Overhand Knot' on page 35). With the fourth group work a Banister Bar (see page 26, two Working Cords and four Filler Cords) 26 in (66 cm) long. Slip one of the large beads over the ends of all six cords and move it up to the Banister Bar. Work the remaining three groups to this point.

43 Simple plant pot hanger in sisal

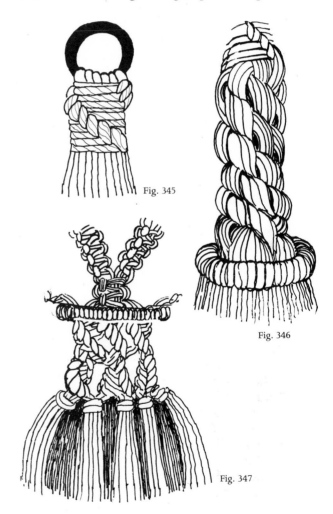

Fig. 345

Fig. 346

Fig. 347

145

6. Using the six strands of one group, divide these into two sets of three cords (two long ones and one shorter one). With the short cord-end in the centre as Filler Cord and the two longer ones on the outside as Working Cords, in turn, knot two Banister Bars, each 21 in (53 cm) long. Repeat with the cords coming from the remaining three beads.
7. With the cords from the right-hand Banister Bar from one bead and the left-hand Banister Bar from the next on the right tie two Flat Knots (see page 22), one below another (two Working Cords and four Filler Cords). Repeat three more times until all Banister Bars are joined.
8. Divide the six cords coming from the Flat Knots into two groups of three strands and knot a Flat Knot Sinnet (see page 33, two longer Working Cords and one shorter Filler Cord) 8 in (20 cm) long with each one in turn, eight in all.
9. Bring the cords from the right-hand Sinnet coming from one set of two Flat Knots together with those from the left-hand Sinnet from the next group on the right and join these with two Flat Knots (two Working Cords and four Filler Cords), one below the other. Repeat three more times until all Flat Knot Sinnets are joined in this way.
10. Push all strands through the second wooden ring (Fig. 347) and move up to the Flat Knots. Using each cord-end in turn and in their right sequence, make one Double Half Hitch Knot over the ring to cover completely.
11. Below the ring and using four cord-ends at a time knot six Banister Bars, each spiralling once only. With the two right-hand strands from one Banister Bar and the two left-hand ones from the next tie another Banister Bar spiralling once only. Repeat five more times.
12. With the right-hand Working Cord from one Banister Bar and the left-hand Working Cord from the next on the right tie one Overhand Knot (see page 35). Repeat five more times until all Banister Bars are joined in this way.
13. Cut all ends to the required length and, if wished, unravel these into separate strands to give a fluffy tassel.

Sisal wall decoration with dried flowers and grasses
(Plate 44, right)
Finished length: 26 in (65 cm)

MATERIAL   Coloured sisal (2½–3 mm)   4 cords, each 4½ yards (4.10 m) long
                  2 cords, each 2¼ yards (2.05 m) long   Dried flowers and grasses
                  4 cords, each 6 yards (5.50 m) long

METHOD
1. Place the two 2¼-yard (2.05-m) cords together and measure 1 yard (90 cm) from one end. At this point tie a temporary Overhand Knot (see page 35) over both strands (Fig. 348). Pin the knot to the board with the longer cord-ends down. Work a Single Chain (see page 33) of twenty-four knots. Remove work from board, fold the chain in half, untie the temporary Overhand Knot and pin the loop to the board with the four cord-ends down.
2. Fold one of the 6-yard (5.50-m) cords in half and place the midway point behind the four vertical cords, just below the ends of the Single Chain (Fig. 349). Pin this cord on the right of the vertical strands and make a vertical Double Half Hitch Knot (see page 31) over these with the left-hand end (Fig. 350).

146

3. Fold one of the $4\frac{1}{2}$-yard (4.10-m) cords in half and place the midway point behind the four vertical cords, just below the vertical Double Half Hitch Knot. Pin the cord on the right and work another vertical Double Half Hitch Knot over the four centre strands, using the left-hand end.
4. Work as 3.
5. Work as 2.
6. Work as 2.
7. Work as 3.
8. Work as 3.
9. Work as 2.
10. Counting from the top use the first four cords on the left to make a Flat Knot Sinnet (see page 33) thirteen knots long. Repeat with the first four cords on the right.
11. From the next group of four cords on either side of the vertical centre line use the fourth (last) one on the right and left respectively as Working Cords and make one Flat Knot (see page 81) over the four centre strands. Put the two cords up and out of the way.
12. Bring down the next cord from either side (third) and use these as Working Cords to make a second Flat Knot over the four centre strands, immediately below the previous one. Leave a small half circle on either side before tightening the knot. Put the cord-ends up and out of the way.
13. With the next two cords from above (second) work a third Flat Knot over the four centre strands, leaving slightly larger half circles on either side. Put the ends up and out of the way.
14. Bring down the last two cords and make one more Flat Knot over the four centre strands, leaving still larger half circles at the sides. Tighten and pin.
15. Now attach the two side Sinnets to the centre strands by curving these inwards and using each of the four strands from either side in turn as Working Cords to make Flat Knots over the centre cords, starting from the top. After each completed Flat Knot put the ends of the Working Cords up and out of the way. There should now be eight strands on either side of the centre cords.
16. Repeat from 10. and work this pattern five more times.
17. Make one Bead Knot (see page 44) seven Flat Knots long using the four centre strands, then knot the side Sinnets thirteen Flat Knots long and attach to the centre cords in the usual way, just below the Bead Knot.
18. Knot two more complete patterns, but before attaching the cords from the last two Sinnets place the four strands on either side of the centre line as additional Filler Cords together with the normal four. Now make one Flat Knot over all twelve cords with the first cord from the Sinnets on either side. Put the Working Cords from this Flat Knot with the Filler Cords and make a Flat Knot over fourteen strands with the next two cords from the Sinnets on either side. Continue using two more Filler Cords in this way until all four Flat Knots are completed. Knot off the left-hand Working Cord together with one Filler Cord using an Overhand Knot (see page 35) and repeat on the right.
19. Cut the ends of the tassel evenly then unravel all cords to give individual strands. Dampen these slightly, hold the tassel in place with rubber bands and remove when dry to avoid untidy ends. (Compare the right-hand tassel which has been treated in this way with that on the left, Plate 44).

20. Finally, decorate with dried flowers or fir cones anchored through the sides of the Bead Knot and held in place by oversewing or with a little glue.

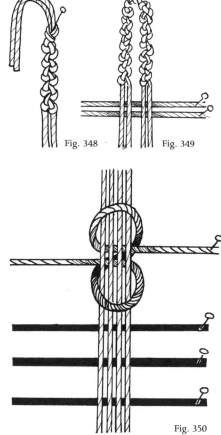

Fig. 348   Fig. 349

Fig. 350

44 Two sisal wall decorations with natural materials and beads

Sisal wall decoration on ring with dried grasses and beads
(Plate 44, left)
Finished length: 33 in (83 cm)

MATERIAL   Coloured sisal ($2\frac{1}{2}$–3 mm)   Dried grasses or flowers
12 cords, each 7 yards (6.40 m) long   7 beads, about $\frac{3}{4}$ in (2 cm)
1 wooden or bamboo type ring, about 4 in   diameter with fairly large
(10 cm) diameter   holes

METHOD
1. Fold each of the twelve cords in half and mount onto the ring with Lark's Head Knots (see page 20).
2. Starting from the left work a Flat Knot Sinnet (see page 33) five knots long with the first four strands, a Flat Knot Sinnet of three knots with the next four cords and one of two knots with the third group of four strands.
3. Work the twelve cords on the right in the opposite way, starting with a Flat Knot Sinnet five knots long on the outside right.
4. Bring the cord on the outside left round a pin and place it as Filler Cord horizontally over all remaining strands on the right. Using each strand in turn make a row of Horizontal Cording (see page 28) over it, starting from the left.
5. *Bring the cord on the outside left round a pin and place it diagonally over the next five strands on the right, sloping from left to right. Using each of the five cords in turn work a row of Diagonal Cording (see page 29) over it, starting from the left.
6. Place the next cord on the left diagonally over the four strands on the right and work a second row of Diagonal Cording over it with each strand in turn, starting from the left.
7. Work the next group of six cords on the right in the opposite way: Bring the cord on the outside right of this group round a pin and place it diagonally over the five strands on the left, sloping from right to left. Using each of the five strands in turn, make a row of Diagonal Cording over it, starting from the right.
8. Place the next strand on the right diagonally over the four cords on the left and work a second row of Diagonal Cording over it with each strand in turn, starting from the right. With the four Filler Cords from the diagonal lines make one Flat Knot (see page 22) to join and pin.
10. Work the twelve cords on the right to this point in an identical way to match the left-hand side.
11. Using the fourth cord from the centre on the left and right respectively tie one Collective Flat Knot (see page 24) over the six centre strands. Pin.
12. Place the left-hand Filler Cord from the Flat Knot on the left diagonally over the five strands on the left and using each cord in turn make a row of Diagonal Cording over it, starting from the right.
13. Using the next cord on the right (first Working Cord from previous row) place this diagonally over the five strands on the left and work a second row of Diagonal Cording over it with each strand in turn, starting from right, including previous Filler Cord.
14. Place the right-hand Filler Cord from the Flat Knot above diagonally over the five strands on the right and using each cord in turn make a row of Diagonal Cording over it,

149

starting from the left. Place the next cord on the left diagonally over the five strands on the right and using each strand in turn work a second row of Diagonal Cording over it, starting from the left (the strands from the Collective Flat Knot should be kept in their right order).

15. Work the twelve cords on the right in an identical way to match the left-hand side.
16. Slip a bead over the two centre cords to join the diagonal lines.
17. With the four centre strands from the left-hand section tie one Flat Knot. Using the two left-hand cords from this Flat Knot and the two strands on the left make another Flat Knot and similarly with the two right-hand cords from the Flat Knot and the two cords on the right. Work one more Flat Knot over the four centre strands (two from the Flat Knot on the left and two from the one on the right).
18. Work right-hand section to match.
19. Repeat from * 5. twice more (the first Filler Cord from the centre comes from the bead). Work a third pattern from * 5. to 15. only.
20. Bring the cord on the outside right round a pin and place it horizontally over all strands on the left. Using each cord in turn, make a row of Horizontal Cording over it, starting from the right.
21. With four cords at a time make six Flat Knot Sinnets, each five knots long right across all strands.
22. Bring the cord on the outside right round a pin and place it horizontally over all remaining strands on the left. With each cord in turn work a row of Horizontal Cording over it, starting from the right.
23. Divide the cords into two groups of twelve strands and work the left-hand section first. Bring the cord on the outside right of this group round a pin and place it diagonally over the eleven strands on the left. Using each cord in turn make a row of Diagonal Cording over it, starting from the right. Place the next strand on the right diagonally over the eleven cords on the left and using each one in turn, make a second row of Diagonal Cording over it, starting from the right.
24. Work the right-hand group of twelve cords in the opposite way.
25. With the four centre cords, two from the right and two from the left, tie one Flat Knot. Using the two left-hand cords from this Flat Knot and the two strands on the left make another Flat Knot and similarly with the two right-hand cords from the centre Flat Knot and the two strands on the right.
26. Continue in this way, making a Flat Knot Diamond, i.e. a row of three Flat Knots next, alternating with the previous one, then a row of four and one of five Flat Knots. Find the four centre cords of this last row and work a Flat Knot Sinnet of about six knots, including the one already tied, to form a Bead Knot (see page 44). In the next row leave out the first two and the last two cords and work four Flat Knots over the remaining strands. Always leaving out two more strands on either side make a row of three Flat Knots, then one of two and one single Flat Knot over the four centre strands.
27. Bring the Filler Cord on the outside left round a pin and place it along the diagonal line formed by the Flat Knot section, sloping from left to right. Using each strand in turn, work a row of Diagonal Cording over it, starting from the left and including the two left-hand strands from the Flat Knot at the centre point.
28. Using the next cord on the outside left, place it diagonally along the previous row of

Cording and work a second row of Diagonal Cording immediately below the first one, starting from the left and including the previous Filler Cord at the end.

29. Work right-hand side to match.
30. Starting from the outside left, make a Flat Knot Sinnet five knots long with the first four strands, a Flat Knot Sinnet of three knots with the next four cords and just one Flat Knot over the next three strands (one Filler Cord only). Work right-hand section to match.
31. Bring the cord on the outside left round a pin and place it horizontally over all strands on the right. Make a row of Horizontal Cording over it, using each strand in turn and starting from the left.

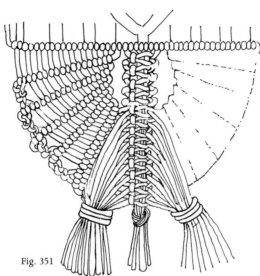

Fig. 351

32. For the fan-shaped ending use the Fig. 351 as a guide. Place the tenth cord from the left as Filler Cord at a slight angle over the nine strands on the left (not fully diagonal). Using each cord in turn make a row of Cording over it, starting from the right. Make a Single Chain (see page 33) of three knots with the two cords on the outside left. Bring the next cord on the right from this group of ten at a slightly steeper angle than the one before over the nine strands on the left. Again work a row of Cording with each strand in turn, starting from the right. Continue in this way until you have five rows of Cording.
33. Work the ten cords on the outside right in the opposite way.
34. With the four centre cords make a Flat Knot Sinnet with Overhand Knot Side Picots (see page 34) four Flat Knots long.
35. Using the four strands from the Sinnet as Filler Cords and one strand from either side as Working Cords, make one Flat Knot. Put the Working Cords up and out of the way. Repeat eight more times always using the next cord from either side as Working Cords. Knot off the four centre strands with one Overhand Knot (see page 35).
36. Bring down the left-hand Working Cords from the vertical line of Flat Knots and using the Filler Cord from the last row of Cording at the side make three Collecting Knots (see page 51) over the nine strands, taking the end over the back of the three knots and pushing it down the centre with a needle to form part of the tassel. Work the right-hand

151

set of cords in the same way. Apply a little fabric glue at the back of the Collecting Knots if necessary.

37. Unravel all cord-ends and dampen, holding the tassels in place with rubber bands until dry to avoid untidy ends. Remove bands and cut all ends in a straight line or to a point. (Compare the right-hand tassel which has been treated in this way with that on the left. Plate 44.)

38. Using the Bead Knot as anchorage point, trim with grasses and beads, holding these in place by oversewing from the back of work.
(Fir cones and coloured balls could be used at Christmas time.)

45 Napkin rings in fine parcel string

Napkin rings

MATERIAL   Thick crochet cotton or fine parcel twine
For each ring: 29 cords, each 33 in (85 cm) long
1 cord, 66 in (1.70 m) long
3 cords, each 10 in (25 cm) long, for trimmings
plastic waste pipe, $1\frac{1}{2}$ in ($3\frac{3}{4}$ cm) diameter, 2 in (5 cm) long

6 beads
Coloured self-adhesive plastic material
Coloured lining material, about 3 × $8\frac{1}{2}$ in (8 × 22 cm)

152

METHOD

1. Cut the plastic piping into 2-in (5-cm) lengths with a saw.
2. Cover each ring with plain coloured self-adhesive plastic material.
3. Cut twenty-nine cords, each 33 in (85 cm) long and one cord 66 in (1.70 cm) long.
4. Fold the long cord in half and place the loop round the piece of plastic piping, fairly near the top. Tie the ends together with a temporary double knot (holding cord).
5. Fold twenty-eight of the 33-in (85-cm) cords in half and in turn set onto the holding cord with Lark's Head Knots (see page 20).
6. Untie the temporary double knot in the holding cord and let the two ends overlap right over left and left over right. Set the twenty-ninth cord onto the double holding cord with one Lark's Head Knot. Secure this point with a paper clip or clothes peg (Fig. 352).
7. Using the right-hand end of the holding cord as Filler Cord, place it horizontally to the right over the Working Cords, just below the Lark's Head Knots. With each Working Cord in turn make one Double Half Hitch Knot (see page 28) over the holding cord to form a row of Horizontal Cording (see page 28) right around the ring. Tighten the left-hand end of the holding cord before taking it into the Cording then end with the two strands from the twenty-ninth cord.
8. With the two ends from the holding cord as Working Cords make one Flat Knot (see page 22) over the two ends from the twenty-ninth strand and then a second one with the same cords immediately below. Using four strands at a time repeat making Flat Knot Sinnets (see page 33), each two knots long, right round the ring.
9. In the second row alternate this two Flat Knot pattern by using the two right-hand cords from one Flat Knot and the two left-hand ones from the next, again working one Flat Knot below another, as before.

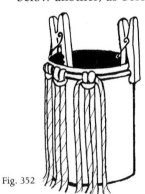

Fig. 352

Fig. 353

LOWER EDGE

Fig. 354

10. Keep alternating in this way until you have six rows of alternate two Flat Knot pattern, gradually pushing the knotting up so that the beginning of the work is level with the edge of the ring.
11. Find the longest end from the original holding cord and place it round the ring as Filler Cord. Using each Working Cord in turn, make a row of Horizontal Cording over it, right round the ring, from left to right. With the second end from the original holding cord as Filler Cord, work another row of Horizontal Cording close to the previous one, starting from the left (Fig. 353).

153

12. Using a needle thread the end of the last Filler Cord through the loop at the beginning of the row to join.
13. Spread a layer of glue over the inside of the serviette ring, push the cord-ends down the centre and align these neatly next to each other (Fig. 354). Trim ends.
14. When dry, line the ring to conceal the cord-ends. A relatively easy way is to stick a piece of felt along the inside. For a more professional look use coloured lining material which is first sewn onto the knotting along the top and then attached to the lower edge.
15. For the trimmings: Thread three cords, each 10 in (25 cm) long through the knotting, at a convenient point in the centre of the ring. Tie three and three ends together with a double knot. Thread one bead over each single cord-end and move up in position. Hold in place with an Overhand Knot (see page 35) and trim.
Note: The number of beads used for each serviette ring could vary for each person in order to make these more easily recognizable.

Dog collar and lead
(Plate 40 on page 131)

COLLAR   finished length for small dog: 15 in (38 cm)

MATERIAL   Cotton twine (about $1\frac{1}{2}$–2 mm)   1 small buckle $\frac{5}{8}$ in ($1\frac{3}{4}$ cm)
            2 cords, each 2 yards (1.80 m) long   1 half ring $\frac{5}{8}$ in ($1\frac{3}{4}$ cm)
            1 cord, $1\frac{1}{2}$ yards (1.35 m) long   1 small ring $\frac{5}{8}$ in ($1\frac{3}{4}$ cm) diameter
            2 cords, each 4 yards (3.65 m) long

METHOD
  1. Fold the two 2-yard (1.80-cm) cords in half and pin the loops next to each other on the board.
  2. Using the two strands on the outside as Working Cords make a Flat Knot Sinnet with Overhand Knot Side Picots (see page 35) 3 in ($7\frac{1}{2}$ cm) long (Fig. 355).
  3. On the reverse side thread the $1\frac{1}{2}$-yard (1.35-m) cord through the lower half of the last Flat Knot, pull the ends even and use these as extra Filler Cords. Place the two Working Cords with the Filler Cords.
  4. Fold the two 4-yard (3.65-m) strands in such a way that one end measures $\frac{3}{4}$ yard (70 cm) and the other $3\frac{1}{4}$ yard (2.95 m). Pin one on each side of the Filler Cords, just below the last Flat Knot, with the longer ends on the outside. The long ends are now the Working Cords and there should be eight Filler Cords in the centre.
  5. Work a Flat Knot Sinnet with Overhand Knot Side Picots until the work measures 9 in (23 cm) from the beginning. Insert the ring (Fig. 356) between the Filler Cords then continue the Sinnet for another 5 in (13 cm). Slide the half ring between the Filler Cords and then the small buckle (Fig. 357). 3 in ($7\frac{1}{2}$ cm) from the last Flat Knot fold all Filler Cords back onto the reverse side of work. This may be done over a small piece of cardboard to form a loop. Temporarily slide the half ring and buckle up to the fold.
  6. Continue working the Sinnet for one more inch ($2\frac{1}{2}$ cm) (over a double layer of Filler Cords) then open the loop and work the Sinnet over the top half first. Four knots from where the loop opens slide the half ring along the Filler Cords up to the last knot then

154

hold in position with four Flat Knots (see page 22) to complete the top layer of the loop. The small buckle remains in the fold (Fig. 358).

7. Cover the back of the loop by working Flat Knots over it. At the point where the Filler Cords are double sew the two Working Cords through the back of work and cut off ends. Stick the two layers of the loop together with fabric glue.

8. Trim all Filler Cords.

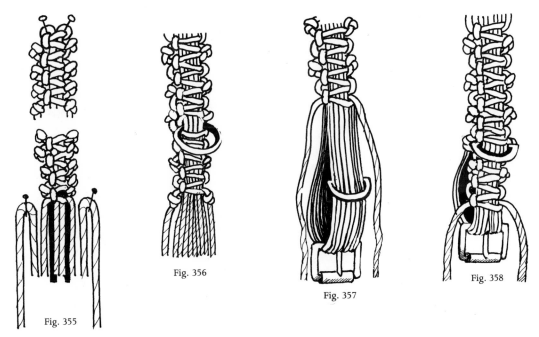

Fig. 355

Fig. 356

Fig. 357

Fig. 358

LEAD   finished length 52 in (1.30 m)

MATERIAL   3 cords, each $3\frac{1}{2}$ yards (3.20 m) long   2 cords, each 14 yards (12.80 m) long
                                                                    1 dog lead clasp

METHOD
1. Push the three $3\frac{1}{2}$-yard (3.20-m) cords through the ring of the dog lead clasp and pull ends even (Fig. 359).
2. Push the two 14-yard (12.80-m) cords through the same ring in such a way that one end measures $1\frac{3}{4}$ yards (1.60 m) and the other $12\frac{1}{4}$ yards (11.20 m).
3. *With the two long ends on the outside right and left respectively knot a Flat Knot Sinnet with Overhand Knot Side Picots $9\frac{1}{2}$ in (24 cm) long.
4. Work a Banister Bar (see page 26) twisting three times.
5. Repeat from * twice more.
6. Knot one more section of Flat Knot Sinnet with Overhand Knot Side Picots.
7. 8 in (20 cm) from the end of this Sinnet fold all Filler Cords over onto the back of work, thereby forming a loop. Tie the cords together with a piece of yarn in order to keep the two layers apart.

155

8. Cut off the ends of the folded Filler Cords at the point of the last Flat Knot and glue the two layers together for about 2 in (5 cm), leaving out the two Working Cords. Hold the glued part in place with adhesive tape until dry.
9. Using the two Working Cords make a Banister Bar over the glued portion then knot all round the loop with Flat Knots and Overhand Knot Side Picots (Fig. 360). Knot off each of the Working Cords with an Overhand Knot (see page 35) and using a needle thread the ends into the back of the Sinnet. Trim. (Fig. 360.)

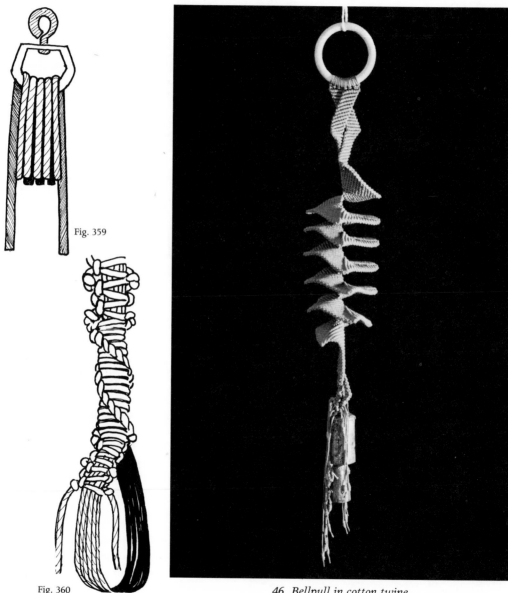

Fig. 359

Fig. 360

46 Bellpull in cotton twine

156

Bellpull

Finished length: 30 in (75 cm)

MATERIAL   Cotton twine ($1\frac{1}{2}$–2 mm)   1 wooden ring, $3\frac{1}{2}$ in (9 cm) diameter
                8 cords, each $16\frac{1}{2}$ yards (15 m) long   2 bells

METHOD

1. Fold each cord in half and set onto the wooden ring with Lark's Head Knots (see page 20).
2. Divide the sixteen Working Cords into two groups of eight. Put the right-hand set up and out of the way.
3. Working with the left-hand group make one Flat Knot (see page 22) using the four cords on the outside left.
4. Bring the strand on the outside left round a pin and place it horizontally over the remaining seven cords on the right. Using each strand in turn work a row of Horizontal Cording (see page 28) over it, starting from the left. *Bring the next cord on the left round a pin and horizontally over the remaining seven strands on the right. Make another row of Horizontal Cording over it with each cord in turn, starting from the left. Repeat ten more times from * until there are twelve rows of Cording. The sides of the knotting should now slope from left to right (see 'Working Zig-Zags' on page 57).
5. Bring back the last Filler Cord on the right, round a pin, and place it horizontally over the remaining seven strands on the left. Make a row of Horizontal Cording over it with each strand in turn, starting from the right. **Bring the next strand on the right round a pin and place it horizontally over the remaining seven strands on the left. Work another row of Horizontal Cording over it with each cord in turn, starting from the right. Repeat ten more times from ** until you have twelve rows of Cording sloping from right to left.
6. Put this set of eight cords up and out of the way and bring down the second group of eight strands. Make a Flat Knot with the four cords on the outside right then work the zig-zag pattern in the opposite direction, bringing the cord on the outside right over the strands on the left to make the first row of Horizontal Cording.
7. Bring down the first zig-zag section then overlap the two twice, right over left.
8. Bring the Filler Cord on the outside left round a pin and place it horizontally over the fifteen strands on the right (Fig. 361)). Work a row of Horizontal Cording over it with each cord in turn, starting from the left.
9. Turn the work slightly to the right so that the last row of Cording is on the diagonal, sloping from left to right.
10. *Bring the next cord on the outside left round a pin and diagonally over the remaining strands on the right. Work a row of Diagonal Cording (see page 29) over it using each strand in turn, starting from the left and leaving out the Filler Cord from the previous row at the end. Repeat from * thirteen more times. The left-hand edge should be straight with the right-hand edge sloping from right to left, ending in a point.
11. Turn the work to the right so that the straight vertical side edge now lies horizontally across the top with a diagonal line running from the point on the left down to the right.
12. Bring the Filler Cord from the point on the left round a pin and place it along the diagonal line formed by the previously worked Cording. Using each strand in turn, make a row of

Diagonal Cording over it, starting from the left. Continue as for the previous section, using the cords on the outside left in turn as Filler Cords and leaving out the previous Filler Cord on the right in each row. Work down to a point then turn the knotting to the right again. Knot a third section, starting with the cord from the point on the left as Filler Cord for the first row.

13. Continue knotting triangles until you have six complete rounds, i.e. twenty-four triangles. (After the third triangle the work will start to overlap and the knotting is done layer upon layer to form a cube shape. Pin the first layer to the board and all subsequent ones to the layer immediately below.)

14. When the last triangle is completed remove all pins and pull the layers apart to form a kind of spiral. Starting from the top turn each layer over in turn so that the reverse side of the Cording faces downwards.

15. Pin the last triangle back to the board, right side up, with all the Filler Cords on the right. Now continue each corded line to the end, i.e. use the Filler Cord from the first row to make a Double Half Hitch Knot (see page 28) over the Filler Cord from the second row. Taking the two cords from the second row in turn, make two Double Half Hitch Knots over the Filler Cord from the third row. With the three strands from the third row in turn, make three Double Half Hitch Knots over the Filler Cord from the fourth row, with the fourth strand from the fourth row in turn, make four Double Half Hitch Knots over the Filler Cord from the fifth row, etc. until all rows are completed right to the end (fifteen rows in all).

16. Divide the sixteen strands into two groups of eight and put the right-hand set up and out of the way. Using the four left-hand cords from the group on the left make six rows of Cording zig-zag fashion, using in turn each strand from the outside left as Filler Cords and including the Filler Cord from the previous row at the end. When the six rows are completed bring the Filler Cord on the outside right round a pin and use it as first Filler Cord for a row of Cording from right to left. Using the next strand on the outside right work one more row of Cording zig-zag fashion.

17. Knot the four right-hand cords from the first group in the opposite way, taking the strand on the outside right as the first Filler Cord. Cross the right-hand zig-zag over the left. With the cord on the outside left as Filler Cord work a row of Cording using each of the seven remaining strands in turn and inserting the larger bell between the third and the fourth knot. Knot off two cords at a time with Overhand Knots (see page 35). Work a Coil Knot (see page 43) on each cord-end at varying lengths. Trim the ends and let the Coil Knots hang over the bell.

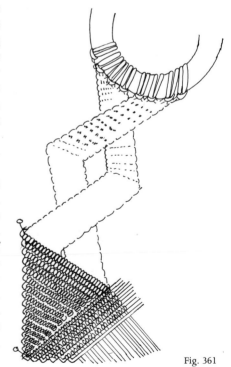

Fig. 361

158

18. Bring down the right-hand group of eight cords and proceed as for the left, but work four zig-zags of six rows with each group of four cords in turn, changing direction at the points and ending with two rows of Cording on each set of four strands. Finish as for the group on the left, inserting the second bell between the third and the fourth knot. Knot off ends and work Coil Knots as before.

Wall hanging
(Colour Plate H)
Size (without hanging up cord): 4 ft × 15 in (1.15 m × 38 cm)

MATERIAL 5-ply jute (3½ mm) white (bleached) and brown
2 wooden rods or bamboo canes about 18 in (46 cm) long
28 white cords, each 8½ yards (7.75 m) long
4 brown cords, each 10 yards (9.10 m) long
13 brown cords, each 34 in (85 cm) long

2 brown cords, each 70 in (1.80 m) long
4 brown cords, each 26 in (65 cm) long, for outlining diamonds
2 brown cords, each 5 yards (4.55 m) long, for hanging up cord
4 oval wooden beads, 2 in (5 cm) long

METHOD
1. In turn, fold each of the white cords in half and set onto one of the wooden rods with Lark's Head Knots (see page 20). Use Fig. 362 as a working diagram.
2. Place the four brown 10-yard (9.10 m) cords together, find the midway point, and position this in the centre of the wooden rod, just below the mounted Lark's Head Knots, with the two ends of the brown cords horizontally out to the left and right respectively. The four brown strands now become the Filler Cords for a row of Horizontal Cording (see page 28). About 2 in (5 cm) to the left of the white cords tie a temporary Overhand Knot (see page 35) over all four brown cords and pin this knot securely to the board. Starting from the left and using each of the white cords in turn, make a row of Horizontal Cording over the brown strands, right across the line (one Double Half Hitch Knot with each white strand), tightening the Lark's Head Knots above as you go along.
3. Using four white cords at a time work a row of two Flat Knots, one below another (fourteen in all).
4. Leaving out the first two and the last two cords and using four cords at a time, make one row of single Flat Knots.
5. Work as 3.
6. With the four brown strands on the outside left work a Double Chain (see page 33) about seven knots long. Repeat on the outside right.
7. Place five 34-in (85-cm) cords together, find the midway point and position this between and just below the seventh and eighth Flat Knot of the last row, with the two ends horizontally out to the left and right respectively (these brown cords now become Filler Cords as before). Again tie a temporary Overhand Knot over all five strands on the outside left and pin the knot securely.

8. Starting from the left and using each of the brown strands from the Double Chain first and then each of the white strands in turn, work a row of Horizontal Cording over the brown Filler Cords, as before, ending with the four brown cords from the Double Chain on the outside right.

9. Using four cords at a time work the Alternate Flat Knot Pattern (see page 25) to the shape shown in Fig 362 (●), providing the outlines for the top half of the two small diamonds to follow.

10. Starting with the diamond on the left, tie one Flat Knot with the four centre strands (top corner). Use the left-hand Working Cord from that Flat Knot as Filler Cord, place it diagonally from right to left along the diagonal line of Flat Knots on the left. With each cord from the Flat Knots in turn and starting from the right, make a row of Diagonal Cording (eight knots) (see page 29).

11. Find the left-hand Filler Cord from the centre Flat Knot, place it diagonally over the eight cords from the previous row of Diagonal Cording and, using each of the eight strands in turn, work a second row of Diagonal Cording, just below the previous one.

12. Using the right-hand Working Cord from the centre Flat Knot at the top as first Filler Cord and then the right-hand Filler Cord from that Flat Knot as second Filler Cord, work two rows of Diagonal Cording sloping from left to right to complete the top half of the left-hand diamond.

13. Work the top half of the right-hand diamond to match.

14. Starting on the outside left, leave out the first two cords, then make one Flat Knot with the next two strands and the two Filler Cords from the diamond. Use the two right-hand Filler Cords from the diamond and the next two cords on the right and make one Flat Knot. Work the right-hand diamond in the same way.

15. Slip a bead over the ends of the two centre strands in each diamond and move up to a central position.

16. Starting on the outside left, find the right-hand Working Cord from the last Flat Knot (left-hand corner of diamond), place it diagonally as Filler Cord across the eight strands on the right, sloping from left to right, and, using each of the eight strands in turn, work a row of Diagonal Cording over it, starting from the left (eight knots).

17. Find the Filler Cord from the Flat Knot in the left-hand corner and place it diagonally over the eight cords from the last row of Diagonal Cording. Using each of the eight strands in turn, work a second row of Diagonal Cording immediately below the previous one, starting from the left.

18. Knot two rows of Diagonal Cording sloping from right to left, using the Working Cord from the Flat Knot in the right-hand corner as the first Filler Cord and then the left-hand Filler Cord from that Flat Knot as second Filler Cord to complete the diamond.

19. Work the right-hand diamond to match.

20. Join the four cords from the two diagonal lines of both diamonds with one Flat Knot each (lower corner).

21. Now fill in around the diamonds with Alternate Flat Knot Pattern to the shape shown in Fig. 362 (x), at the same time providing the shape for the top half of the large diamond in the centre.

22. Work one Flat Knot with the four centre strands (top corner of large diamond). Use the cords from this Flat Knot as Filler Cords for the Diagonal Cording along the top half of the

large diamond in the same way as for the small ones, but taking eighteen strands into each row instead of only eight.

23. Divide the thirty-six cords from the diamond into four groups of nine strands (ignore the Filler Cords) and tie one large knot as shown in Fig. 362.

24. With the brown cords on the outside left and right in turn, knot two Double Chains about thirty knots long or to the same length as the white section.

25. Place one end of three 34-in (85-cm) cords and one end of the two 70-in (1.80-m) cords together. Leave about 9 or 10 in (23 to 26 cm) for the tassel then place the strands from left to right horizontally across the work. Knot a row of Horizontal Cording over the brown strands, as before, taking in the four cords from the Double Chain first and then the first ten white strands. Now find the ends of the two long cords from the group of brown Filler Cords and use these as Working Cords to make a Flat Knot Sinnet about twenty knots long (or to reach the left-hand corner of the large diamond). Push this Sinnet under the first and last groups of nine vertical cords from the large knot in the centre, then complete the line of Horizontal Cording, starting with the two Filler Cords from the Diagonal Cording and ending with the four brown strands from the Double Chain on the right.

26. Bring the right-hand cord from the Horizontal Cording (left-hand corner) diagonally across the eighteen left-hand strands from the large knot, sloping from left to right and, using each strand in turn, work a row of Diagonal Cording over it. Use the second cord on the left from the Horizontal Cording as second Filler Cord and make another row of Diagonal Cording immediately below the previous one. Work the right-hand side of the large diamond to match.

27. Fill in around the large diamond with Alternate Flat Knot Pattern to the shape shown in Fig. 362 (■), then work two more small diamonds, as before, again filling in around these with Alternate Flat Knot Pattern to the shape marked (▲). Below the last two diamonds there should be ten rows of Alternate Flat Knots.

28. Work two Double Chains of about thirty-two knots (or to the same length as the white section) using the brown cords on the outside left and right respectively.

29. With five brown 34-in (85-cm) strands as Filler Cords make a further row of Horizontal Cording right across the work, as before.

30. Using four cords at a time work fourteen Flat Knot Sinnets, each eight knots long, right across all strands.

31. Work two Double Chains with the brown cords on the outside left and right respectively (about eleven knots).

32. Attach all cords to the second wooden rod with Double Half Hitch Knots (Cording), starting with the four brown cords from the Double Chain on the left and ending with the four brown strands from the Double Chain on the right.

33. Knot off four cords at a time with Overhand Knots (see page 00) then unravel each cord into separate strands to obtain a fluffy fringe. Trim ends to required length.

34. Trim the side tassels to the required length.

35. To work a hanging up cord, place the two 5-yard (4.55-m) cords together, fold in half and attach to one end of the wooden rod at the top with one Lark's Head Knot. Knot a Double Chain about 26 in (66 cm) long, then attach to the other end of the rod before knotting off at the back.

36. Using each of the four brown 26-in (65-cm) cords in turn, outline the four small diamonds with running stitches, starting from the back through the space immediately below the Flat Knot at the lowest point of the diamonds and ending by pushing the yarn to the back through the same space. Sew ends into the back of work.

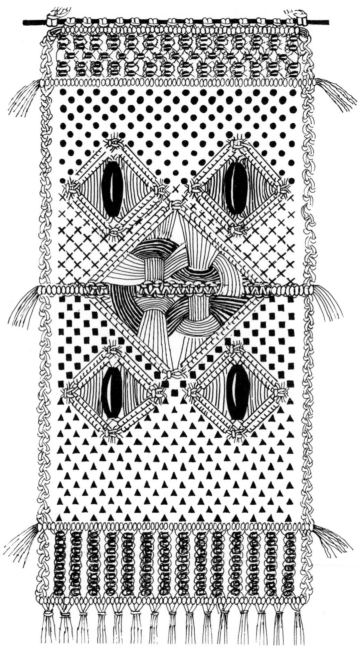

Fig. 362

Lantern

Finished length: 24 in (60 cm)

MATERIAL   5-ply natural jute (3 mm)
3 metal rings, 8 in (20 cm) diameter
2 metal rings, 6 in (15 cm) diameter
1 metal ring, 4 in (10 cm) diameter
1 wooden ring, 2 in (5 cm) diameter
28 cords, each $5\frac{1}{4}$ yards (4.70 m)
long

7 cords, each $4\frac{1}{2}$ yards (3.80 m) long
10 wooden beads, $1\frac{1}{4}$ in (3 cm) diameter
1 wooden bead, $1\frac{1}{4}$ in (3 cm) diameter, to be positioned over light fitting
4 oval shaped beads, about 1 in ($2\frac{1}{2}$ cm) long

METHOD

1. In turn, fold fourteen of the $5\frac{1}{4}$-yard (4.70-m) cords in half and set onto the small wooden ring with Lark's Head Knots (see page 25).
2. Using four cords at a time work four rows of Alternate Flat Knot Pattern (see page 25), knotting in the round and gradually increasing the spaces between the individual knots and rows. From this point onwards it is not possible to use the knotting board. Ideally the lantern should be free-hanging as you work on it.
3. Slip all cord-ends through one of the 6-in (15-cm) metal rings and place it along the base of the last row of Flat Knots. From below and using each strand in turn attach the four cords from one Flat Knot to the wire with Double Half Hitch Knots (see page 28) then repeat with all strands from the remaining Flat Knots, leaving spaces between each attached section (seven in all).
4. Using two $5\frac{1}{4}$-yard (4.70-m) cords for each space, in turn fill these in by folding the strands in half, placing the fold under the ring with the loop showing just above the wire. From below make one Double Half Hitch Knot with each cord-end to cover the wire completely (Fig. 363).
5. Divide the cords into four groups of fourteen strands. Still knotting in the round and working with one group first * make one Flat Knot over the four centre strands and position it about $\frac{1}{4}$ in ($\frac{1}{2}$ cm) below the wire. Place the cord on the outside left from this group diagonally over the next six strands on the right, as Filler Cord, and using each cord in turn make a row of Diagonal Cording (see page 29) over it, starting from the left. Using the strand on the outside right as Filler Cord, place this diagonally over the next six cords on the left. Work a row of Diagonal Cording over it with each strand in turn, starting from the right. The two diagonal lines should meet in the centre. Work the remaining three groups of fourteen cords in the same way, starting from *.
6. Thread one oval bead over the two Filler Cords in the centre of each group to join the diagonal lines.
7. Working with the cords between two beads now, ** tie one Flat Knot with the four centre strands at the top. Using the two left-hand strands from this Flat Knot and the next two cords on the left tie a second Flat Knot. With the two right-hand strands from the centre Flat Knot and the next two cords on the right make another Flat Knot. Using the four centre strands work two Flat Knots, one below another, and similarly with the four cords to the left and to the right of these two Flat Knots. Leave the two strands on the outside left and right respectively unworked and tie two Flat Knots with the remaining eight

163

cords. Tie one more Flat Knot over the four centre strands, thereby bringing this section to a point. Repeat from ** three more times with the cords between the remaining beads.

8. *** Place the right-hand Filler Cord from one bead from left to right over the next six cords on the right, along the diagonal line provided by the Flat Knots and using each of the six cords in turn work a row of Diagonal Cording over it, starting from the left.

9. Bring the left-hand Filler Cord from the bead over the next six cords on the left, along the diagonal line provided by the Flat Knots and using each strand in turn make a row of Diagonal Cording over it, starting from the right. With the four centre strands between the two diagonal lines work a Flat Knot Sinnet (see page 33) three knots long. Repeat from *** three more times, starting with the Filler Cords from the remaining beads.

10. Slip one 6-in (15-cm) ring over all cord-ends and position it just below the Flat Knot Sinnets and ends of the diagonal lines. From below work one Double Half Hitch Knot over the wire with each strand in turn to cover the ring completely.

11. Using four cords at a time work three rows of Alternate Flat Knot Pattern (see page 25) right round, slightly increasing the spaces between the individual knots and rows.

12. Insert one 8-in (20-cm) ring below the last row of Flat Knots, as before, leaving small spaces between each group of attached cords.

13. Fold one of the 4½-yard (3.80-m) cords in half and place the fold behind one of the Flat Knots just above the last inset wire ring. Bring one end of this cord out on the left and the other on the right of the Flat Knot, below the wire. With the left-hand end from this strand make one Double Half Hitch Knot over the ring, between the already attached cords from this Flat Knot and the Flat Knot on the left (Fig. 364). Repeat with the right-hand end of the cord, again between two Flat Knots. Repeat 13. six more times, placing the fold of one 4½-yard (3.80-m) strand behind every alternate Flat Knot above the ring and bringing the ends out to the left and right respectively before attaching these to the wire. The 8-in (20-cm) ring should now be completely covered.

14. Starting at any point along this ring **** use three cords to tie one Flat Knot (two Working Cords and one Filler Cord). Slide one 1¼-in (3-cm) bead over the end of the Filler Cord, moving it up to the Flat Knot. Use Fig. 365 as a guide. With the two Working Cords tie a Banister Bar (see page 26) 7 in (18 cm) long over the Filler Cord coming from the bead. Leave the next four strands along the ring unworked, then tie one Flat Knot with the next three cords. Insert one 1¼-in (3-cm) bead, as before, then use the two Working Cords to tie a Flat Knot Sinnet 7 in (18 cm) long over the Filler Cord coming from the bead. Leave the next four strands unworked, then repeat from **** four more times right round.

15. With each group of four unworked cords and ignoring the worked Sinnets tie one Flat Knot, then work six more rows of Alternate Flat Knot Pattern, in the round, over all forty strands, gradually reducing the spaces between the individual knots and rows.

16. Slip the 4-in (10-cm) ring over all forty cord-ends, move it up to the last row of Flat Knots, then insert the ring using Double Half Hitch Knots, as before.

17. Below the inset ring knot nine rows of Alternate Flat Knot Pattern, gradually increasing the spaces between the individual knots and rows.

18. Slip one 8-in (20-cm) ring over all cord-ends, including those from the Sinnets, then attach all strands in turn to the wire using Double Half Hitch Knots (alternately three cords from one Sinnet and then four strands from one of the Flat Knots from the Alternate Flat Knot Pattern in the centre).

164

47 Lantern worked in jute

165

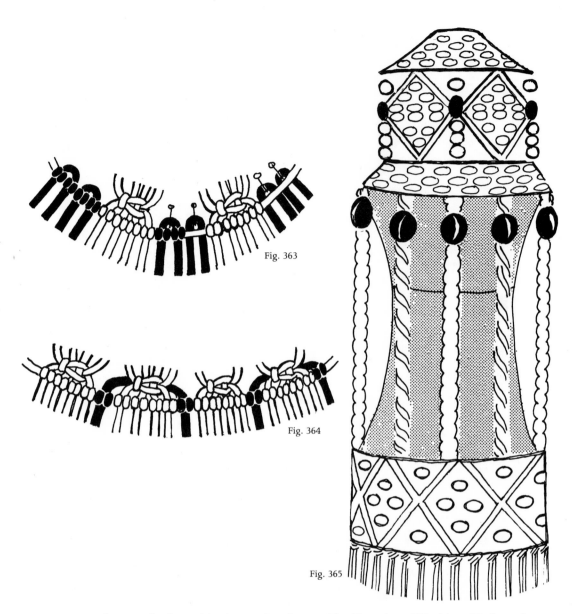

Fig. 363

Fig. 364

Fig. 365

19. Use any four cords along this ring and make one Flat Knot (two Working Cords and two Filler Cords). Place the third strand on the left of this Flat Knot diagonally over the next four cords on the right (two from the ring and two from the Flat Knot). Using each of these strands in turn make a row of Diagonal Cording over it, starting from the left. Bring the third cord on the right of the Flat Knot diagonally over the next four strands on the left (two from the ring and two from the Flat Knot) and using each cord in turn work a row of Diagonal Cording over it, starting from the right. To join the two diagonal lines the left-hand Filler Cord remains a Filler Cord and the right-hand Filler Cord becomes a

166

Working Cord. Use the right-hand strand to make one Double Half Hitch Knot over the left.

20. Repeat this pattern six more times, right round the ring (ten cords for each pattern).
21. Between two patterns find the four cords at the top (two from the Diagonal Cording on the left and two from the right) and tie one Flat Knot. Using the left-hand two strands from this Flat Knot and the next two strands on the left tie a second Flat Knot. Similarly, make one Flat Knot with the two right-hand cords from the first Flat Knot and the next two strands on the right. Make one more Flat Knot over the four centre strands.
22. Now work the lower half of the diamond. Still using the same Filler Cord from the Diagonal Cording on the left, place this diagonally from left to right over the next four strands on the right (two from each Flat Knot) and using each cord in turn work a row of Diagonal Cording over it, starting from the left. Place the Working Cord from the join on the right diagonally over the four cords on the left (two from each Flat Knot) and using each strand in turn make a row of Diagonal Cording over it, starting from the right.
23. Knot 22. six more times right round the work.
24. Find the four centre strands between each of these patterns and tie one Flat Knot.
25. Slip the last 8-in (20-cm) ring over all cord-ends and insert, as before, using Double Half Hitch Knots.
26. Knot off two cords at a time with Overhand Knots (see page 35). Leave about 4 in (10 cm), then cut all ends to form tassels. To make a fluffier fringe unravel each cord-end into single strands.
27. Push one bead about $1\frac{1}{4}$ in (3 cm) over the flex and on top of the light fitting. This will make the point at the top stand up. According to the knotting tension a larger bead may be required.

Small shopper
Size without handles: 12 × 11 in (30 × 28 cm)

MATERIAL   2 bag handles with curved base, 8 in (20 cm) at widest point   Cotlon No. 4 or cotton yarn (2 mm)
For each half: 32 cords, each 4 yards (3.65 m) long   2 cords, each 60 in (1.55 m) long, Filler Cords for base
4 cords, each 1 yard (90 cm) long, extra Filler Cords

METHOD
1. To work the first half fold each of the thirty-two cords in half and mount onto one bag handle with Lark's Head Knots (see page 20): if using Cotlon, tie an Overhand Knot into each cord-end to avoid excessive fraying.
2. Using four cords at a time work sixteen Flat Knot Sinnets (see page 33), three knots long.
3. With the two strands on the outside left work a Single Chain (see page 33) five knots long. Repeat with the two cords on the outside right. Using four cords at a time knot fifteen Flat Knot Sinnets, three knots long, over the remaining strands, thereby alternating the Sinnet pattern.
4. Work as 2.

5. Work as 3.
6. Work as 2.
7. Knot an identical second half to this point.
8. Working on one half first, use one of the 1-yard (90-cm) cords, leave about 6 in (15 cm) from one end and make a temporary Overhand Knot (see page 35) at this point. Pin this knot just to the left and below the first Flat Knot Sinnet on the outside left. Place the longer end horizontally along the base of the Flat Knot Sinnets and use it as Filler Cord to make a row of Horizontal Cording (see page 28) over it with each strand from the Flat Knot Sinnets in turn, starting from the left.
9. Place the second half of the bag next to the first, right side up, bring the same Filler Cord as before horizontally over all the strands from the second half, just below the Sinnets, and continue the row of Horizontal Cording, using each strand in turn, leaving the last cord on the outside right unworked (Fig. 366). Remove work from board, put one half of the bag on top of the other, right sides out. Place the two ends of the Filler Cord over and against each other. Using the last cord left unworked make one Double Half Hitch Knot (see page 28) over the double Filler Cord to join the front to the back (Fig. 367). Pull the two ends of the Filler Cord out to the right and left respectively to tighten. Sew the ends up into the Sinnets on the reverse side of work. Trim ends.
10. From this point the bag is worked in the round. Cut a double layer of corrugated cardboard (from a box) 11 in (28 cm) wide and about 10 in (25 cm) long. Use this as a base to work over. Push the cardboard up on the inside of the bag so that the top is about 1 in ($2\frac{1}{2}$ cm) above the corded line. Pin. A small cushion could be inserted between the layers of cardboard to give more bulk.
11. *Starting from the left, on one side of the bag, make three Flat Knots (see page 22) over the first twelve strands, using four cords at a time. Leave the next eight cords unworked. Make six Flat Knots over the next twenty-four strands, leave the next 8 cords unworked. Work three Flat Knots over the next twelve strands, turn bag over and repeat from *.
12. Working on one Flat Knot section first bring this to a point by leaving out the first two and the last two cords in each row (six decreasing rows of Alternate Flat Knots (see page 25) in all). Bring the three remaining Flat Knot sections to a point in the same way.
13. Using the two outside cords from each group of eight unworked strands make one Collective Flat Knot (see page 24), four in all. Pin.
14. Along the diagonal edges of each Flat Knot section use two cords at a time to make one Double Half Hitch Knot, starting from the top (first cord is Working Cord, second Filler Cord). There should be six individual Double Half Hitch Knots along each side.
15. Bring the right-hand Working Cord from one Collective Flat Knot diagonally as Filler Cord along the row of Double Half Hitch Knots on the right, sloping from left to right, and work a row of Diagonal Cording (see page 29) over it, using each strand from the Double Half Hitch Knots in turn, starting from the left (twelve knots).
   Place the right-hand Filler Cord from the Collective Flat Knot diagonally as Filler Cord across the twelve strands on the right and using each of these in turn, work a second row of Diagonal Cording over it, immediately below the previous one, starting from the left (twelve knots).
   Work two more rows of Diagonal Cording below this last one, using the next two Filler Cords from the Collective Flat Knot as Filler Cords (twelve knots each).

16. With the remaining four cords from the Collective Flat Knot make four rows of Diagonal Cording sloping from right to left, using the left-hand Working Cord from the Collective Flat Knot as the first Filler Cord.

17. Using the cords from the remaining three Collective Flat Knots in turn, repeat from 15. three more times.

18. Along the sloping edges of the diagonally corded sections and using two cords at a time, work six Double Half Hitch Knots, as before, starting from the top (first cord Working Cord, second cord Filler Cord).

19. With the four cords from the first Double Half Hitch Knot on the left and right respectively (top corner), work one Flat Knot. Using the two left-hand strands from this knot and the next two cords on the left from the second Double Half Hitch Knot, work a second Flat Knot. Using the two right-hand cords from the first Flat Knot and the next two strands on the right from the second Double Half Hitch Knot work one Flat Knot. Continue in this way, taking in two more cords from the left and from the right in each row, until you have a row of six knots in the sixth row. Knot an identical row to the sixth.

20. Leaving out the first two and the last two strands in each row bring the Alternate Flat Knot Pattern to a point until one Flat Knot remains.

21. Along the sloping sides from the Flat Knot sections again use two cords at a time and in turn make six Double Half Hitch Knots along each side, starting from the top.

22. Repeat from 19. three more times right round the bag.

23. Find the left-hand Filler Cord from one of the diagonally corded sections, sloping from left to right. Place this horizontally from left to right, as Filler Cord, over the next seven strands on the right. Using each one in turn, work a row of Horizontal Cording over it, starting from the left (Fig. 368). Bring the same Filler Cord round a pin and place it horizontally over the seven strands on the left. Using each strand in turn make a second row of Horizontal Cording immediately below the first one. Work two more rows of Horizontal Cording in this way, using the same Filler Cord all the time and bringing it back round a pin on the outside left and right respectively. Work three more horizontally corded sections in the same way right round the bag.

24. Place the left-hand Filler Cord from one of the horizontally corded sections diagonally from right to left, as Filler Cord, along the sloping line of six corded knots on the left.
   With the twelve strands from the Double Half Hitch Knots in turn work a row of Diagonal Cording over it, starting from the right. Using the next three strands from the Horizontal Cording in turn, as Filler Cords, make three more rows of Diagonal Cording immediately below the first one.
   With the remaining four cords from the Horizontal Cording in turn work four rows of Diagonal Cording, sloping from left to right, using the right-hand cord from the Horizontal Cording as first Filler Cord. Repeat 24. three more times, right round bag.

25. With the eight cords from the diagonally corded sections make one Collective Flat Knot, as before. Repeat three more times, right round the bag.

26. Using two cords at a time make six Double Half Hitch Knots along each of the sloping lines from the Diagonal Cording, then fill in with Alternate Flat Knot Pattern, starting with one Flat Knot, taking in two more cords from the left and right respectively in each row, until there are six Flat Knots in the last row.

27. Use one of the 1-yard (90-cm) cords as Filler Cord and work a row of Horizontal Cording right round the bag, joining the two ends in the same way as for the previously set in strand.
28. Use four cords at a time and work Flat Knot Sinnets three knots long right round the bag.
29. Set in one more 1-yard (90-cm) cord to make a row of Horizontal Cording right round the bag, as before, then join in the last 1-yard (90-cm) strand, but starting on the opposite side. This will give an ending of two horizontally corded lines.

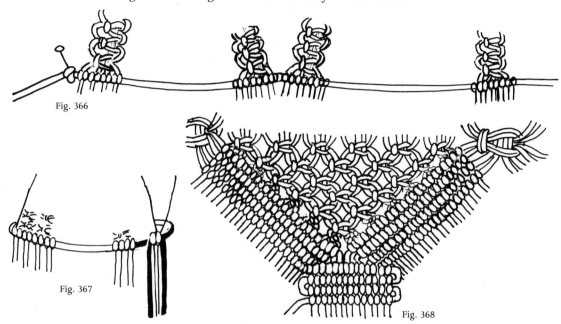

Fig. 366

Fig. 367

Fig. 368

To work base: On the outside left and right respectively tie ten cords together with a temporary Overhand Knot (see page 35) (five strands from the front and five from the back). Measure about 5 in (13 cm) from one end of one 60-in (1.55-m) cord and tie an Overhand Knot at this point. Pin this knot on the left of work and place the strand horizontally, as Filler Cord, across all remaining cords (between the two temporary Overhand Knots). Using each strand in turn make a row of Horizontal Cording over it, immediately below the previous Cording, starting from the left (Fig. 369). Bring the same Filler Cord round a pin and horizontally back over all strands. Work a second row of Cording over it with each cord in turn, starting from the right. Bring the same Filler Cord back, round a pin, and make one more row of Horizontal Cording from left to right and then a last one from right to left. Turn work over and work the second side in the same way.

Turn bag inside out. Starting from the left, take one cord from the front section and one from the back. Knot these together with an ordinary double knot. Always using one strand from the front and one from the back tie double knots right across the row. Working on one side of the join first, take about six cord-ends, make a short plait, tie the ends together with a piece of thread and sew the plait to the base (Fig. 370). Using about six strands at a time repeat right across the line. Work the opposite side of the join in the same way. Trim all ends.

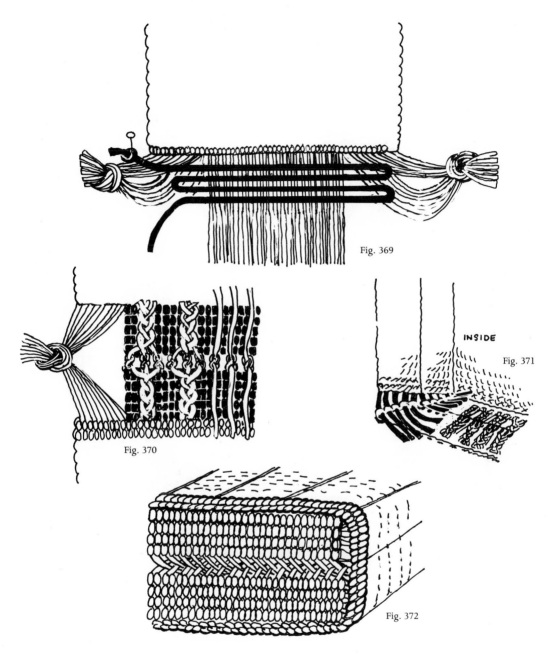

Fig. 369

Fig. 370

Fig. 371

INSIDE

Fig. 372

Release the ten cords on either side tied into temporary Overhand Knots. Push the individual strands one by one through the edges formed by the Cording (Fig. 371), using a needle or crochet hook. Knot two ends together at a time, including the two strands from the extra Filler Cords. Again make small plaits, tie with thread and sew to the base of the bag. Trim ends, and turn the bag right side out (Fig. 372).

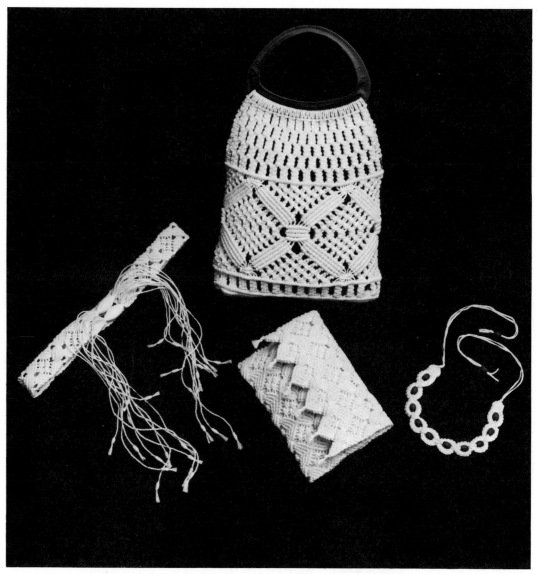

48 Shopper in Cotlon, evening purse, matching belt (not described) and choker

Envelope evening purse
Size: 6 × 9 in (15 × 23 cm)

MATERIAL White Cotlon No. 5 or white or coloured tubular rayon
29 cords, each 5½ yards (5 m) long

1 cord, 6 yards (5.50 m) long, holding cord
lining material

METHOD

1. Measure 3 yards (2.75 m) from one end of the holding cord, tie an Overhand Knot (see page 35) at this point and pin the knot to the board. Measure 9 in (23 cm) from the pin horizontally to the right, tie an Overhand Knot at this point and again secure to the board with a pin.
2. Fold each of the 29 cut cords in half and set onto the holding cord, between the two pins, with Lark's Head Knots (see page 20).
3. Bring the left-hand end of the holding cord round a pin and as Filler Cord horizontally from left to right across all the remaining strands. Using each of the Working Cords in turn and starting from the left, make a row of Horizontal Cording (see page 28) right across the line. Use Fig. 373 as a working diagram.
4. Bring the Filler Cord from the row of Cording round a pin, place it diagonally as Filler Cord over the next strand on the left and use this as Working Cord to make one Double Half Hitch Knot (see page 28) over the Filler Cord.
5. Place the first cord on the outside left as Filler Cord diagonally from left to right over the second strand and use this to make one Double Half Hitch Knot over the Filler Cord.
6. Using four cords at a time work a complete row of Flat Knots (see page 22) between the two Double Half Hitch Knots at either end.
7. Place the left-hand Working Cord from the first Flat Knot on the left as Filler Cord diagonally over the two strands from the Double Half Hitch Knot on the outside left, sloping from right to left, and using each one in turn, make two Double Half Hitch Knots over it, starting from the right.

   Place the next cord from the Flat Knot as Filler Cord diagonally over the three strands on the left (counting the previous Filler Cord as the third) and using each cord in turn, make a row of Diagonal Cording (see page 29) over it, starting from the right.

   Place the next cord from the Flat Knot as Filler Cord diagonally over the four strands on the left and work a third row of Diagonal Cording, as before, including the previous Filler Cord on the outside left. Work a fourth row of Diagonal Cording in the same way, using the last cord from the Flat Knot as Filler Cord and including the Filler Cord from the previous row on the outside left.
8. Place the right-hand Working Cord from the second Flat Knot on the left as Filler Cord diagonally over the two left-hand cords from the third Flat Knot and make one Double Half Hitch Knot over it with each cord in turn, starting from the left (two knots).
9. Place the left-hand Working Cord from the fourth Flat Knot on the left as Filler Cord diagonally over the two right-hand strands from the third Flat Knot and use these in turn to make two Double Half Hitch Knots over it, starting from the right.

   To join the two diagonal lines the left-hand Filler Cord remains a Filler Cord and the right-hand Filler Cord becomes a Working Cord to make one Double Half Hitch Knot over the Filler Cord. Place the next cord from the fourth Flat Knot diagonally, as Filler Cord, over the next three strands on the left (two from the Cording and one Filler Cord). Use each of these in turn to make a row of Diagonal Cording over it, starting from the right.

   Place the next cord from the second Flat Knot diagonally, as Filler Cord over the next four strands on the right (three from the Cording and one Filler Cord) and make a row of Diagonal Cording over it with each strand in turn, starting from the left.

173

Place the next strand from the fourth Flat Knot diagonally, as Filler Cord, over the next four cords on the left and work a row of Diagonal Cording over it with each of these in turn, starting from the right. Place the next cord from the second Flat Knot diagonally as Filler Cord across the five strands on the right and work a row of Diagonal Cording over it with each of these in turn, starting from the left. Bring the last cord from the fourth Flat Knot diagonally as Filler Cord over the next five strands on the left and make a row of Diagonal Cording over it with each of these in turn, starting from the right. Bring the last cord from the second Flat Knot diagonally as Filler Cord over the next six strands on the right and make a row of Diagonal Cording over it with each of these in turn, starting from the left.

10. Work one more of these heart-shaped patterns using the cords from the next three Flat Knots on the right.

11. Work two more heart-shaped patterns with the cords from the next two groups of three Flat Knots but reversing these, i.e. knot the first row of Diagonal Cording from the left and right respectively as before, but join the two diagonal lines by using the left-hand Filler Cord as Working Cord to make one Double Half Hitch Knot over the right-hand Filler Cord and continue from there alternating the knotting direction first from the left and then from the right and so on.

12. On the outside right place the right-hand Working Cord from the remaining Flat Knot across the two cords from the Double Half Hitch Knot on the outside right and use these in turn to make a row of Diagonal Cording over it (two knots).
     Bring the next cord from the Flat Knot diagonally across the three strands on the right and make a row of Diagonal Cording immediately below the previous one (three knots).
     Make two more rows of Diagonal Cording to match the left-hand side (four and five knots).

13. Find the four centre cords on the left, between the first half and the first full heart-shaped pattern (two from each), and make one Flat Knot. Using the two left-hand cords from this Flat Knot and the next two strands on the left tie one Flat Knot. Using the two right-hand cords from the first Flat Knot and the next two cords on the right make one Flat Knot. Work one more Flat Knot over the four centre strands (two from the Flat Knot on the left and two from the right). Repeat this pattern of four Flat Knots four more times, i.e. between each set of two heart shapes.

14. Bring the Filler Cord from the last row of Cording on the left round a pin and place it diagonally as Filler Cord, from left to right, over the next five strands on the right. Use each of these in turn to make a row of Diagonal Cording over it, starting from the left.
     Bring the next cord on the outside left round a pin and place it diagonally as Filler Cord over the next four strands on the right. Work a row of Diagonal Cording over it with each one in turn, starting from the left (four knots).
     Bring the next cord on the outside left round a pin and place it diagonally as Filler Cord over the next three strands on the right. Work a row of Diagonal Cording over it with each one in turn, starting from the left (three knots).
     Bring the next cord from the left round a pin and as Filler Cord diagonally across the next two strands on the right. Work a last row of Diagonal Cording over it (two knots).
     Use the four Filler Cords to make one Flat Knot which should be on the diagonal.

15. Bring the Filler Cord from the first full heart shape on the left diagonally as Filler Cord

across the next five strands on the right (one from the Cording and four from the Flat Knots). Using each cord in turn make a row of Diagonal Cording over it, starting from the left and continuing the previous line (five knots).

Use the second cord on the left from this line of Cording and place it diagonally as Filler Cord over the next five strands on the left (one from the Cording and four from the Flat Knots). Work a row of Diagonal Cording, using each one in turn, starting from the right (five knots). Place the first cord on the right from this last row as Filler Cord diagonally over the next five strands on the right and make a row of Diagonal Cording over it, starting from the left (five knots).

Place the first cord on the left from this last row diagonally as Filler Cord across the next four strands on the left and make a row of Diagonal Cording, starting from the right (four knots).

Place the first cord on the right from this last row of Diagonal Cording across the next four strands on the right and make a row of Diagonal Cording, starting from the left (four knots).

Place the first cord on the left from this last row diagonally as Filler Cord across the next three strands on the left and make a row of Diagonal Cording, starting from the right (three knots).

Bring the first cord on the right from this last row diagonally as Filler Cord across the next three strands on the right and make a row of Diagonal Cording, starting from the left (three knots).

Bring the first cord on the left from this last row diagonally as Filler Cord across the next two strands on the left and make a row of Diagonal Cording, starting from the right (two knots).

16. With the four Filler Cords on the left tie one Flat Knot. Repeat with the four Filler Cords on the right.

17. Work the next inverted heart shape on the right in the same way and reverse the procedure for the next two heart shapes on the right, as before. Knot the half shape on the outside right in the opposite way to the left-hand one.

18. The two Flat Knots in between the heart shapes are now used as the start for one Berry Knot (see page 46). Work five in all.

19. Between the Berry Knots tie one Flat Knot with the four cords coming from the heart-shaped patterns (four in all).

20. Using the second cord on the outside left place it diagonally as Filler Cord over the strand on the outside left and use this to make one double Half Hitch Knot sloping from right to left. Bring the same Filler Cord round a pin and diagonally from left to right over the next strand on the right. Use this to make one more Double Half Hitch Knot, sloping from left to right, over the Filler Cord.

21. Repeat on the outside right in the reverse way.

22. Repeat the pattern from 7. five more times, finishing with one more row of single heart shapes.

23. Knot off the two centre strands from each heart shape and similarly the two outside cords from the half shapes with one Overhand Knot (see page 35) and trim ends, leaving a short tassel. Cut the remaining cords to about $\frac{1}{2}$ in ($1\frac{1}{4}$ cm). Fold back the ends and sew neatly to the reverse side of the heart shapes with thread.

24. Line the bag and fold in such a way that the pattern on the flap corresponds with the work beneath, then sew the sides together.

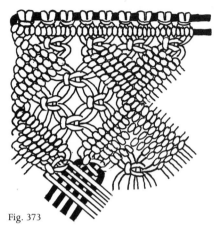

Fig. 373

49 *Evening purse with Berry Knots in Cotlon*

Cavandoli make-up bag
(Colour Plate B)

MATERIAL	Coloured dish-cloth cotton White dish-cloth cotton		Lining material 1 zip fastener, 7 in (18 cm)
For each side:	32 cords, each 1¾ yards (1.60 m) long		2 cords, each 2 yards (1.80 m) long
For front:	1 white cord about 10 yards (9.10 m) long wound into a ball		2 cords, each 20 in (50 cm) long, for sewing the sides together

METHOD
Back:
1. Fold the two 2-yard (1.80-m) cords in half and pin the halfway point to the board. Measure 4 in (10 cm) horizontally out to the left and right of this point and secure the two cords in both places (holding cords). Remove centre pins.
2. Take two of the 1¾-yard (1.60-m) cords, fold in half and make an Overhand Knot Picot (see page 48, Figs. 136–137) at the halfway point. Place this under the two holding cords on the outside left so that the Picot shows just above. Pin Picot. With each of the four Working Cords from this Picot in turn make one Double Half Hitch Knot (see page 28) over the holding cords, starting from the left (Horizontal Cording).
3. Using two of the 1¾-yard (1.60-m) cords at a time make Overhand Knot Picots, as described above, and set these onto the holding cords in turn, to the right of the already set on Picot.
4. The two ends of the holding cords on the outside left and right respectively are now taken into the work. Tie an Overhand Knot (see page 35) into one end of the white cord and secure this knot with a pin about 4 in (10 cm) to the left of the work, just below the

176

row of Cording. With the white strand as Filler Cord right through and the remaining strands as Working Cords make first a row of Horizontal Cording starting from the left and using each strand in turn. When this row is completed bring the white Filler Cord round a pin and horizontally back across all Working Cords, from right to left. Make a row of Horizontal Cording, using each strand in turn, starting from the right.

5. Continue knotting rows of Horizontal Cording alternately from left to right and right to left until the work measures about $4\frac{1}{4}$ in (11 cm) (twenty-nine rows).

Front:

Work 1. to 4. as for back.

5. Make one more row of Horizontal Cording from left to right.
6. Bring the white Filler Cord round a pin, work eight horizontal Double Half Hitch Knots, starting from the right, then begin the pattern, making a vertical Double Half Hitch Knot (see page 31) with the white cord over one coloured strand at a time, following Fig. 374 on this page (the dark spaces represent a white vertical Double Half Hitch Knot and the blank spaces a coloured horizontal Double Half Hitch Knot—see 'Cavandoli Work' on page 74).
7. When the pattern rows are completed continue making rows of Horizontal Cording from right to left and left to right until the work measures about $4\frac{1}{4}$ in (11 cm) or the same as the back.
8. Place back and front together, wrong sides out. Starting at one end and using two cord-ends from the front and two from the back tie an ordinary double knot. Repeat right across the row until all cord-ends are tied, thereby joining the base of the front to the back.
9. With about six cord-ends at a time make small plaits, tie the ends with a Collecting Knot (see page 51), using the longest strand of each group, then use the same strand to sew the ends of the plaits to the inside of the bag (half the plaits to the front and half to the back).
10. To line the bag pin and sew the lining material initially to the sides only, starting to stitch about 1 in ($2\frac{1}{2}$ cm) below the top edges and leaving the white side loops free.
11. Fold the work in half and join the sides by oversewing through the white loops, using separate cords (see page 64). Neatly conceal the ends on the inside.

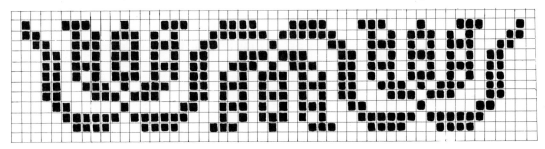

Fig. 374

12. Insert the zip fastener along the top and attach a small tassel.
13. Now stitch the top edges of the lining to the material of the zip, leaving enough space below the metal for the zip to work smoothly.

Cavandoli handkerchief pocket

MATERIAL   Coloured dish-cloth cotton   Lining material
               White dish-cloth cotton

For each   14 cords, each 1½ yards (1.35 m) long
side: 2 cords, each 1 yard 22 in (1.45 m)
               long

For front: 1 white cord, about 4½ yards (4.10 m   2 cords, about 14 in (35 cm) long, for
               long   sewing sides together

METHOD
Back:

1. Fold the two 1-yard 22 in (1.45 m) cords in half and pin the halfway point to the board. Measure 2 in (5 cm) to the left and to the right of these pins and secure the two strands at both points (holding cords). Remove centre pins.
2. Using two of the 1½-yard (1.35 m) cords at a time make Overhand Knot Picots (see page 48, Figs. 136–137) and set these onto the holding cords as for the make-up bag.
3. Work as 4. for the make-up bag.
4. Continue knotting rows of Horizontal Cording from left to right and right to left alternately until the work measures about 3½ in (9 cm) or twenty-six rows.

Front:

     Work 1., 2. and 3. as for back.
4. Make one more row of Horizontal Cording from left to right.
5. Bring back the white Filler Cord, round a pin, work five horizontal Double Half Hitch Knots with the white cord over the coloured strands for the design following Fig. 374, and horizontal Double Half Hitch Knots for the background.
6. When the pattern rows are completed continue making rows of Horizontal Cording from right to left and left to right respectively until the work measures 3½ in (9 cm) or the same as the back.
7. Work 8. and 9. in the same way as for the make-up bag.
8. Sew the lining material along all four edges to the wrong side of the work, fold the knotting in half and join the sides by oversewing through the white loops, using separate cords. Neatly conceal the ends on the inside.

Cavandoli spectacle case

MATERIAL   Coloured dish-cloth cotton   Lining material
               White dish-cloth cotton

For each   14 cords, each 2½ yards (2.25 m) long
side: 2 cords, each 2 yards 22 in (2.35 m)
               long

For front: 1 white cord, about 8 yards (7.30 m)   2 Cords, each about 20 in (50 cm)
           long   long, for sewing sides together

METHOD
Back:
1. Fold the two 2-yard 22 in (2.35-m) cords in half and pin the halfway mark to the board. Measure 2 in (5 cm) horizontally out to the left and to the right of these pins and secure the two strands again at both points (holding cords). Remove centre pins.
2. Using two of the $2\frac{1}{2}$-yard (2.25-m) cords at a time make Overhand Knot Picots (see page 48, Figs. 136–137) and set these on as shown for the make-up bag.
3. Work as 4. for the make-up bag.
4. Continue knotting rows of Horizontal Cording from left to right and right to left alternately until the work measures about $7\frac{1}{4}$ in (18 cm) (fifty rows).

Front:
   Work 1., 2., 3., 4. and 5. as for the handkerchief pocket.
6. When the pattern rows are completed continue making rows of Horizontal Cording from right to left and left to right respectively until the work measures $7\frac{1}{4}$ in (18 cm) or the same length as the back.
7. Work 8. and 9. in the same way as for the make-up bag.
8. Work the same as 8. for the handkerchief pocket.

Cat

Length: 18 in (46 cm)

MATERIAL   5-ply jute (3 mm)   1 cord, 9 yards (8.20 m) long, for tail
           8 cords, each $4\frac{1}{2}$ yards (4.10 m) long   1 piece of wood, slightly curved (piece
           8 cords, each 4 yards (3.65 m) long   of branch), about 10 in (25 cm) long
           2 cords, each $1\frac{1}{2}$ yards (1.35 m) long,   2 oval rings, $1\frac{1}{2}$ × $2\frac{1}{2}$ in ($3\frac{1}{4}$ × $6\frac{1}{2}$ cm)
           for side of nose   made from basket cane (about three
           4 cords, each $2\frac{1}{4}$ yards (2.25 m) long,   layers wrapped over each other)
           extra cords for body   2 oval beads for eyes, 1 in ($2\frac{1}{2}$ cm) long
           1 cord, 1 yard (90 cm) long for ad-
           ditional whiskers

METHOD
1. To work left ear, fold two of the $4\frac{1}{2}$-yard (4.10 m) cords in half and place the loops next to each other on the board. Pin and make one Flat Knot (see page 22) over four cords, using the two outside strands as Working Cords and the two centre ones as Filler Cords. Use Fig. 375 as a guide.
2. Fold one of the $4\frac{1}{2}$-yard (4.10-m) cords in such a way that one end measures 2 yards (1.80 m) and the other $2\frac{1}{2}$ yards (2.30 m). Pin the loop to the left and just below the already tied Flat Knot, with the shorter cord-end on the outside left. With these two new strands and the two left-hand cords from the Flat Knot make one Flat Knot over four cords.

50 Cat worked in jute

180

3. Fold one of the 4-yard (3.65-m) cords in half and pin the loop to the right and just below the first Flat Knot. With the two new strands and the two right-hand cords from the first Flat Knot tie another Flat Knot over four cords.
4. In the next row repeat 2. and then 3. with the longer cord-end on the outside left, pinning the loops just below the previous Flat Knots. Make one more Flat Knot over the four centre strands.
5. * Leaving out the first two and the last two strands make two Flat Knots with the remaining eight cords. In the next row work three Flat Knots right across all twelve strands, then repeat from * once more.
6. Work the right ear in the opposite way (longer cords on the right).
7. Place the left-hand end of the branch just below the left ear. Starting from the left and making Double Half Hitch Knots (see page 28) over the branch, attach the ear, using each cord-end in turn.
8. Fold the remaining four 4-yard (3.65-m) cords in half and place each loop in turn under the wood. Pin the loops just above the branch, starting on the right of the set on ear and working to the right. Using each cord-end in turn make one Double Half Hitch Knot over the branch, starting from the left. Attach the right ear to the wood in a similar way to the left. You should now have thirty-two Working Cords.
9. Using four cords at a time make eight Flat Knots (see page 22) right across all strands. Leaving the first two and the last two cords unworked make a row of seven Flat Knots.
10. With the four strands on the outside left knot a Flat Knot Sinnet (see page 33) eleven knots long.
11. Repeat with the four cords on the outside right.
12. Using the cords between the two Sinnets now, make a row of six Flat Knots.
13. Leaving out six cords from the left and right respectively make three Flat Knots over the remaining twelve strands. Leaving out the first two and the last two of these twelve strands work two Flat Knots over the remaining eight cords. Leaving out the first two and the last two cords of these eight strands make a Flat Knot Sinnet three knots long with the remaining four cords. You should now have ten cords on either side of this short Sinnet.
14. Insert the oval rings at a slight angle, slanting towards the centre. The ten cords are first worked over the top half of the oval and then used to cover the lower edge. The knots used are Double Half Hitch Knots (see 'How to insert a ring' on page 66). Slide a bead over the ends of the two centre cords from each eye and move it in position before attaching the strands to the lower edge of the oval.
15. Using the two left-hand cords from the centre Sinnet (three knots) and two strands from the left eye make one Flat Knot, slanting from right to left. With the two right-hand cords from the centre Sinnet and two cords from the right eye make one Flat Knot, slanting from left to right. Use these two Flat Knots for the start of a Berry Knot (see page 46) and work the corded part of the knot with the eight strands provided by the two Flat Knots. Complete the Berry Knot with two Flat Knots, one tied over the four Working Cords and one over the four Filler Cords, to form the nose.
16. Add an extra cord on the left side of the nose by folding one of the 1½-yard (1.35-m) strands in half and pushing the loop from behind through to the front, between the two cords from the eye taken into the Flat Knot and forming part of the Berry Knot. Slip the

cord-ends through the loop and tighten to give an inverted Lark's Head Knot (see page 20). Repeat on the right side of the nose.

17. Using the two new cord-ends from the left side of the nose and the next two strands from the left eye make one Flat Knot. With the next four cords from the left eye make another Flat Knot.

18. Work the right-hand side to match.

19. With the two remaining cords on the outside from the left eye work a Single Chain (see page 33) five knots long. Repeat with the two outside cords from the right eye.

20. Taking the two cords from the Single Chain of the left eye and the next two cords on the right make one Flat Knot. Work another Flat Knot with the next four strands on the right, leaving the last two cords unworked in this row. Work the right-hand side to match.

21. Using the two cords from the Flat Knot on the outside left make a Single Chain of two knots only, work two Flat Knots over the next eight strands and knot the right-hand side to match.

22. Taking the two right-hand cords from the last Flat Knot on the left, nearest the nose, push these horizontally behind the Berry Knot, coming out to the front on the right side of the nose. Similarly, push the two left-hand cords from the last Flat Knot on the right of the nose through to the left. These four strands remain unworked at present and later become part of the whiskers. Put these up and out of the way.

23. Use the two strands from the Single Chain on the outside left and the next two cords on the right, make one Flat Knot and work another one over the next four cords on the right. Work the right-hand side to match.

24. With the right-hand two cords from the Sinnet on the outside left and the next two cords on the right make one Flat Knot, thereby attaching the Sinnet to the centre section. Make two more Flat Knots with the next eight cords on the right, including two from the nose in the second one. Work one Flat Knot over the four centre strands from the nose and knot the right-hand side to match.

25. Starting from the left make a row of Flat Knots right across all strands.

26. Starting from the left, leave out the first two and the last two cords and make a row of Flat Knots over all remaining strands. Use Fig. 376 as a guide from now on.

27. With the four cords on the outside left work a Flat Knot Sinnet twenty-three knots long. Repeat with the four cords on the outside right.

28. Fold one of the 2½-yard (2.25-m) cords in half and push the loop from behind through to the front, over the right-hand cord from the first Flat Knot of the Sinnet. Slip the cord-ends through the loop and tighten to form an inverted Lark's Head Knot. Work right-hand side to match. Work a row of six Flat Knots between the newly inset strands. Using the two new strands on the left and the next two cords from the Flat Knot on the right make one Flat Knot. Work six more Flat Knots in this row, taking the two ends from the new cord on the right into the sixth one.

29. Fold another 2½-yard (2.25-m) cord in half, insert as before but this time over the left-hand strand from the previously inset cord which was then taken into the first Flat Knot on the left. Repeat on the right-hand side of work to match.

30. With the two strands from the new cord on the left and two cords from the next Flat Knot on the right make a Flat Knot Sinnet nineteen knots long. Repeat on right-hand side of work to match.

31. Work six rows of Alternate Flat Knot pattern (see page 25), starting with a row of six Flat Knots.
32. Divide the centre cords between the Sinnets into two groups of twelve strands. Starting with the left-hand set first work thirteen rows of Alternate Flat Knot Pattern, making three knots in the first row and two in the next. Repeat with the second group of twelve cords on the right.
33. With the two right-hand cords from the Sinnet on the outside left and the two left-hand cords from the next Sinnet make one Flat Knot. Make one more Flat Knot over the next four cords, thereby attaching the second Sinnet to the centre portion. Make two more Flat Knots over the next eight strands, leaving out the last two. Work right-hand side to match.
34. Starting from the outside left work a row of five Flat Knots and repeat on the right-hand side.

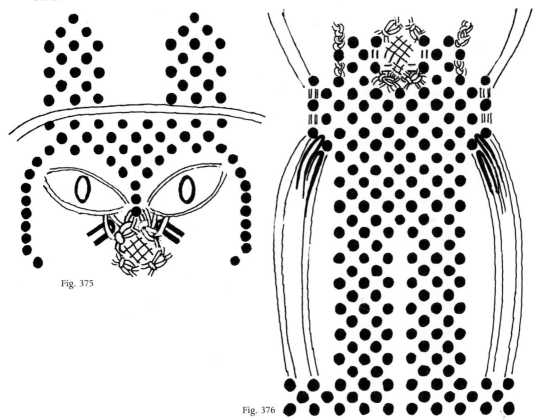

Fig. 375

Fig. 376

To finish off the lower edge of the left half: Place the first cord on the outside left horizontally to the right and make a Half Hitch Knot (see page 31) over it with the second strand. Using the first and the third cord as Filler Cords now and still using the second as Working Cord, make another Half Hitch Knot over both. Gradually taking one more strand from the right to the Filler Cords keep tying Half Hitch Knots with the same Working Cord

183

until all strands from the left half of the cat have been used up and worked over, at the same time cutting out the shortest of the Filler Cords after about every third Half Hitch Knot so that the edge does not become too bulky.

To make the tail: Fold the 9-yard (8.20-m) cord in half and place that point under the loose Filler Cords. Using a needle thread the top end of this strand through the top loop of the last Half Hitch Knot and the second end through the bottom edge of the last Half Hitch Knot. Place the Working Cord for the Half Hitch Knots with the Filler Cords now and with the two ends from the newly inset strand as Working Cords, tie Flat Knots along the edge of the right half of the cat, gradually taking two more strands at a time into the Filler Cords and at the same time cutting out one or two of the shortest Filler Cords so that the tail does not become too thick. Knot the tail tightly which will make it stiff and keep its shape. When all strands from the right half have been used up fold the Filler Cords over and keep tying Flat Knots over the top, not cutting out any more Filler Cords until the tail approaches the left-hand edge of the cat's body. At this point, gradually cut out more Filler Cords so that the tail eventually tapers to a point. Curve the tail upwards and round again (see Plate 50). With four Filler Cords left sew the two ends of the Working Cords into the back of the tail and cut the Filler Cords about $\frac{1}{2}$ in ($1\frac{1}{4}$ cm) from the last Flat Knot to form a small tassel. A stitch will hold the tail-end in place.

To work the whiskers: Unravel the two cords on either side of the nose to give five double strands. Unravel the additional cord of 1 yard (90 cm) and separate two strands. Insert these two strands from one side of the nose to come out on the other, giving an extra double strand on either side. Using two double strands at a time make three Double Chains about $2\frac{1}{2}$ in (7 cm) long on either side of the nose, then knot off with Overhand Knots (see page 35). A stitch may be needed here and there for the whiskers to stay in place.

Macramé-edged mirror

MATERIAL   Crochet cotton or fine string about 130 cords, each 28 in (70 cm) long
1 cord, $4\frac{1}{2}$ yards (4.10 m) long, for Single Chain round mirror
2 cords, each 6 yards (5.50 m) long, for hanging up cord
6 cords, each 21 in (55 cm) long, for tassels
About 23 to 25 beads, $\frac{3}{8}$ in (1 cm)
About 20 metal curtain rings, $\frac{7}{8}$ in ($2\frac{1}{4}$ cm) diameter

Clear drying fabric glue
1 circular mirror, about 7 in (18 cm) diameter (inexpensive mirrors are available from chain stores. The plastic surround has to be removed)
1 piece felt about 10 in (25 cm) square (colour to match beads or contrast)
1 piece thin cardboard about $7\frac{1}{2}$ in (19 cm) square
2 pieces of basket cane, one about 35 in (90 cm) and one about 26 in (66 cm) long

METHOD
1. Place two 28-in (70-cm) cords together, fold in half and make an Overhand Knot Picot at this point (see page 48, Figs. 136–137).
2. Prepare five more sets of two cords in this way.
3. Place the longer piece of basket cane on your knotting board. Push the first Picot under

184

the cane, about 3 in (8 cm) from the left-hand end and pin with the Picot just showing above the cane. Using each of the four cord-ends in turn, work one Double Half Hitch' Knot (see page 28) over the cane, from below and starting from the left. Important: the individual Double Half Hitch Knots along the outer circle are only just to touch each other and must not be moved together tightly. The reason for this is that the same number of cords will later have to cover the inner circle which is smaller. Use Fig. 377 as a working diagram.

4. Set on the other five Picots in the same way, pinning each one next to the previous one, working from left to right.

5. Leave the first two cords on the left unworked. Make a Collective Flat Knot (see page 24) over the next six cords (two Working Cords and four Filler Cords) and pin. Leave the next eight cords unworked and make a further Collective Flat Knot over the next six strands. Pin.

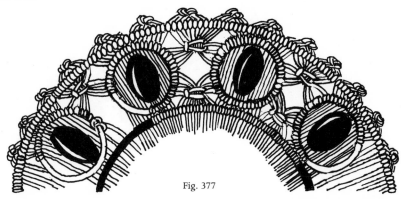

Fig. 377

6. Place one curtain ring over the eight centre cords, between the two Collective Flat Knots, and insert the ring (see 'How to insert a ring' on page 66), starting with the two centre strands of the eight and working in both directions. When all eight cords have been mounted take three strands from the left-hand Collective Flat Knot and set these onto the ring in turn to the left of the already mounted cords. Use three cords from the Collective Flat Knot on the right and set these onto the ring to the right of the already mounted cords. The top half of the ring should now be covered. Push all ends through the ring to the back.

7. Starting on the outside left and then the right respectively cover the lower edge of the ring as shown on page 66, threading one bead over the two centre cords and moving it up inside the ring, before attaching the last two cords to the lower edge. These may have to be passed over the ring with a needle.

8. Set on a further number of Picots, about ten, to give additional Working Cords.

9. Continue working the pattern, leaving out eight cords and making a Collective Flat Knot over the next six, before inserting another ring and bead.

10. When three or four rings have been put in position go back to the first two. Using three cords from the right-hand side of the first and three strands from the left-hand side of the second tie a Collective Flat Knot over six strands (two Working Cords and four Filler Cords). Pin. Repeat between the second and third ring.

185

51 Macramé-edged mirror in nylon fishing twine with beads

11. With a pencil draw the outline of the mirror onto the knotting board and start to curve the work round it, pinning frequently.
12. Place the shorter piece of basket cane along the marked line, just below the rings. About 2 in (5 cm) from the left-hand end and using each strand in turn, attach the eight cords from the first ring onto the cane with Double Half Hitch Knots (see page 28), starting from the left. For the above-mentioned reason the cords on the inner circle must be pushed together very closely.
13. Continue setting on Picots, inserting rings and attaching the cords from the rings and then from the Collective Flat Knots onto the inner circle until you reach the point where the cane needs joining (see 'Useful tips' on page 121). The outer circle is put together first. When the join is dry work over it as before.
14. It is a matter of luck as to whether the number of cords will work out just right to accommodate the ring pattern all the way round (the number of cords depends on slight variations in the thickness of the yarn used, the working tension and the fractional difference in the size of mirrors). It is, therefore, often necessary to knot an improvised pattern between the first and the last ring as illustrated in Plate 51 (the ending is done in Flat Knots, some worked over four and some over three strands before the cords are attached to the inner circle).
15. Join the two ends of the inner basket cane circle as before and when dry work over it in the usual way. Trim all cord-ends to about 1 in ($2\frac{1}{2}$ cm).

To finish: Cut the piece of cardboard to a circular shape, large enough to cover the back of the mirror and the edge of the inner circle. At the back of work apply fabric glue all round the inner circle. Place the cardboard on top. Turn over carefully and weight with a book or similar. When dry remove the book and spread glue all over the cardboard area. Neatly align all cord-ends, one next to the other, in a circular fashion. Apply additional glue over the cord-ends, making sure not to spread it too close to the edge. Now place the mirror on top. Weight with a circular basin, plant pot, etc. placed over a piece of paper or cloth so as not to scratch the mirror.

In the meantime, work the decorative tassels (if used). Take two of the 21-in (55-cm) cords, place these together and tie an Overhand Knot at one end. Pin the Overhand Knot to the board, long ends down, and work a Single Chain (see page 33) about 4 in (10 cm) long. Repeat with the remaining two sets of two 21-in (55-cm) strands. Untie the Overhead Knots on all three chains and weave these in and out of the Flat Knot or other pattern at the base of the mirror. The weaving should be done in a decorative fashion and the ends are left to hang down. Thread beads over the cord-ends, knot off with Overhand Knots to hold in place, then trim all ends. Untwist the individual strands to make small tassels.

To work the hanging up cord: Place the two 6-yard (5.50-m) cords together and fold in half. About 3 in (8 cm) from the fold tie an Overhand Knot over the four cords and pin it to the board with the long ends down. Work a Double Chain (see page 33) with two and two cords to the desired length, which will probably be about 20–24 in (50–60 cm), then leave about 3 in (8 cm) unworked and cut off the ends. From the centre bead at the top of the mirror count three beads to the left. At this point and using a needle thread the cord-ends from one end of the Double Chain in turn through the back of the Cording along the outer circle. Repeat on the other side after untying the temporary Overhand Knot at the beginning of the hanging up cord and cutting the ends open. Glue the cord-ends next to each other, at the back of the

187

cardboard. When dry, spread adhesive all over the cardboard area, a thin line along the edge of the outer circle and a small dab onto each bead. Place the felt on top. Carefully turn the mirror back onto the right side, press down the outer circle and the beads, then weight the centre once more until dry. Finally cut away all surplus felt by trimming along the outer circle at the back of work.

To make a decorative cord round mirror: Fold the $4\frac{1}{2}$-yard (4.10-m) cord in half and pin the loop to the board with the cord-ends down. Work a Single Chain long enough to fit around the edge of the mirror. Push the two cord-ends through the loop at the beginning of the chain (from front to back). Glue a short piece of these ends to the back of the Single Chain and cut off surplus. When dry apply a thin line of adhesive along the edge of the mirror, 2–3 in (5–7 cm) at a time, pinning the decorative cord in place as you go along. Try to keep the knotting and the mirror free from glue. Any adhesive accidentally spread over the mirror may be removed with a razor blade once completely dry.

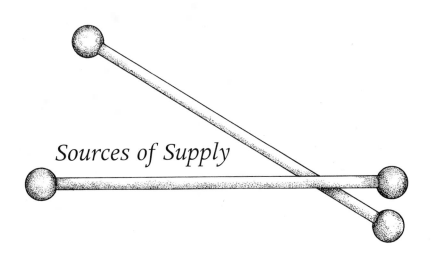

Sources of Supply

The Rope Shop
26 High Street
Emsworth
Hampshire

A perfect knotter's paradise. An outstanding selection of Macramé twines, beads and accessories. Also books. Most efficient mail order service. Retail and wholesale trade.

Mechanical & Model Supplies
39 Kings Road
St. Leonards-on-Sea
Sussex

Very good range of jutes and other yarns as well as accessories.

Inspirations
57 Meadway Precinct
Tilehurst
nr. Reading

Good supply of all basic materials.

Freeman's Hobbies & Handicrafts
77–79 Mayers Walk
Peterborough
Cambs

Range of basic Macramé supplies.

Daedalian Crafts Ltd
18–20 Station Parade
Harrogate
Yorkshire

Stockists of jutes in various thicknesses, synthetic yarns and kits. Also beads.

189

Ellerkers Walmgate York City	Rope merchants also dealing in Macramé supplies.
Bits & Bobs The Craft Centre 46 Church Street Twickenham Middlesex	Range of yarns and accessories.
A & M Crafts Willesden House St. Thomas' Green Haverford West Dyfed Wales	A wide selection of Macramé requirements. Expert service.
Sewing Machines and Needlecraft 7 Linkfield Corner Redhill Surrey	A good range of twines, jutes and other yarns. Also accessories and beads.
Hobby Horse 15–17 Langton Street London SW10	Various jutes and twines. Excellent selection of beads and accessories.
The Handweavers Gallery & Studio 29 Haroldstone Road London E17	Primarily suppliers of weaving requirements but also stocking jutes and twines suitable for Macramé work.
Music and Crafts The Square Forest Row Sussex	Some jutes and twines, also a selection of beads and other accessories.
L. H. Turtle Ltd 6–12 Park Street Croydon Surrey	A variety of jutes and other yarns. Also accessories.
Papersmiths Winchester Street Basingstoke Hampshire	A good selection of Macramé supplies.

Craftworkshop 89 St. Nicholas Market Bristol	Macramé and other craft requirements.
Art Repro 8 De-la-Beche Street Swansea Wales	Various jutes and twines. Also accessories.
Centre Crafts 97 London Road East Grinstead Sussex	General crafts. Some Macramé twines, beads, rug wool, accessories and plant holder pots.
John P. Milner Ltd 67 Queen Street Hitchin Herts	Unusual selection of interesting belt buckles and clasps (will send). Catalogue available.